Contents

Foreword

One day the CEO of a major pharmaceutical company was reviewing the corporation's spreadsheets, when he noticed that the total annual budget for training and development was a phenomenal *$240 million*. That sum, by any standard, is a major investment, but he had no idea what the return was on this investment. The CEO took action: He mandated that the HR department calculate the return-on-investment for all of the training programs. He wanted an evaluation conducted with the same statistical rigor as studies that are done when a new medication is tested for effectiveness.

The results were startling. The company's annual one-week, off-site event for top managers, during which professors from business schools lectured about leadership, had *zero* effect on the actual leadership abilities of these executives. The results were similarly disappointing for the company's main development programs for managers and supervisors: no improvements in job performance and no effects from training. The return-on-investment from these training programs was nil.

The overall message from this company's evaluation was that although some of their training programs did have strong effects, too many did not. The question became, "What distinguishes the programs that work—that actually produce the intended improvements in on-the-job performance—from those that do not?"

That question, in one form or another, is now being asked more frequently of those who design and run training and development programs. The winds of a new, more discerning attitude are sweeping through the training and development industry as customers—those who pay for these programs—want to be sure that they are getting their money's worth.

The answers have always been quite clear when it comes to teaching technical or analytical skills; the classroom model works well for these. Many of these purely cognitive abilities can be learned quickly through reading, through simple rote learning, or by interactive learning on CD-ROM.

When it comes to soft skills, however, the answers are fuzzy. This is the domain of emotional intelligence—recognizing and managing our own feelings and those of others—the fundamentals upon which are built such important organizational competencies as outstanding leadership, customer service, and teamwork.

These are the capabilities that organizations most passionately want to develop in their people, and yet the record in this area has been most uneven. When I wrote *Emotional Intelligence,* I was surprised that even though that book focused mainly on child development and education, more than half of the invitations I received for lectures and consultations came from businesses. That phenomenon led me to write *Working With Emotional Intelligence,* which explores how this range of human ability matters for the world of work and how best to help people improve this range of capability.

As I was writing that book, Cary Cherniss and I founded the Consortium for Research on Emotional Intelligence in Organizations (originally called the Fetzer Consortium, after the foundation that provided the initial funding). One of the consortium's first missions was to sift through the empirical evidence in this domain of ability to identify the synergistic elements that make some training programs effective. This book is the fruit of our efforts.

This book is based on two of the consortium's major activities:

- developing best-practice guidelines for what makes a training program in EI most effective
- identifying model programs that embody many or most of these guidelines.

The best-practice guidelines are based on an exhaustive review of the research on how people actually change and learn in the domain of soft skills, as opposed to technical skills or purely cognitive abilities. The model programs, ably described in this book by Mitchel Adler, represent more than a dozen very different approaches to promoting or developing emotional intelligence. Each has been proven effective through rigorous evaluation studies and has been replicated in different organizations under the guidance of different trainers and coaches. The list is not definitive; the consortium is continuing to identify such programs and add them to a best-practice database.

The consortium is pleased to partner with the American Society for Training & Development in publishing this book for practitioners, the people who have the responsibility to design, to implement, and to evaluate training and development programs. This book provides practitioners with not only the best-practice guidelines for such training but also strong data, making a business case for the importance of emotional intelligence development at all levels in an organization, particularly for leadership.

The book presents the best-practice guidelines, illustrated with examples taken directly from the model programs. In this way, the reader can see immediately in a concrete way how each guideline has been applied. Each model program is described in chapter 3 to help the reader see how the guidelines have been applied in organizations.

The world of training and development has reached a moment of maturity, a time when it is essential that we raise the bar and bring a new measure of exceptional quality to the field. This book can contribute significantly to the training profession's ongoing collective learning to fulfill its mission with ever-greater excellence.

Daniel Goleman

Co-Chair, Consortium for
Research on Emotional
Intelligence in Organizations

Preface

Some time ago we met with the head of a major business school, a man who previously had been a top executive at a *Fortune* 100 company. We began to talk about the qualities that are most important for leadership and personal success in business. He readily agreed that it takes more than technical skill or cognitive competence; motivation and the ability to get along with people really count. When we heard that this business school dean was sold on the idea that soft skills are important, we naturally were curious to learn what his school was doing to help students in the master's degree program acquire them. When we asked, he was taken aback: "Why, we don't do anything," he replied. "People develop those sorts of qualities as children. By the time we get them, they are adults, and there's nothing we can do to help them improve in these areas."

We suspect that this attitude is common. Even if managers and executives recognize the importance of emotional intelligence, they often doubt whether adult workers can improve in this way. Yet, U.S. organizations spend billions every year on training in soft skills. For example, General Electric Company spends $1 billion a year on leadership programs, most of which focus on social and emotional competencies associated with emotional intelligence (Sweeney 1999). In 1997, the American Society for Training & Development conducted a benchmarking survey that revealed that four out of five companies were trying to promote emotional intelligence in their employees.

How can organizations be sure that their investments in time, effort, and money are not being wasted? Can adults really become more emotionally intelligent? If they can, what are the most effective strategies for helping them do so?

To answer these questions, we formed the Consortium for Research on Emotional Intelligence in Organizations, which comprises top researchers from academia, the government, the corporate world, and a leading consulting firm. With funding from the Fetzer Institute, a private foundation, the consortium spent more than two years studying the body of research on competence at work, training and development, and the psychology of personal change. The consortium included Richard Boyatzis, professor of management and associate dean of the Weatherhead School of Management, Case Western Reserve University; Robert Caplan, professor and director of the organizational psychology program, George Washington University; Daniel Goleman, CEO of Emotional Intelligence Services; Marilyn Gowing, director of resources and development, U.S. Office of Personnel Management; Kathy Kram, professor of organizational behavior at Boston University School of Management; Richard Price, professor of psychology, University of Michigan; Mary Ann Re, manager of AT&T corporate employee research; and Lyle Spencer, Hay Group research fellow and CEO of Spencer Research and Technology; and the authors of this book.

The work of the consortium led to the development of this book, which opens with a definition of emotional intelligence and then goes on to describe the growing body of research and experience about how emotional intelligence is essential to achieve individual and organizational success. Twenty-two best-practice guidelines emerged from the consortium's study of model programs and from hundreds of studies on the psychology of behavioral change. These guidelines can aid HRD professionals and managers as they develop methods for helping people become more emotionally intelligent and more effective in the workplace.

The consortium members provided innumerable insights and information for which we are deeply in their debt. Passages from an unpublished manuscript by Daniel Goleman were incorporated into the text with his permission. We also acknowledge the invaluable input of our advisor, Maurice Elias. Maurice had co-chaired a similar consortium that focused on children, and he spent many hours sharing with us the lessons that he and his colleagues had learned. The consortium never would have been so productive without Maurice's ongoing guidance.

We extend special thanks to David Sluyter and Mickey Olivanti of the Fetzer Institute. They not only provided funding for this project, but they also were supportive and understanding whenever we needed their help.

Also, we offer our gratitude to the many individuals who provided information about model programs. The list includes several members of the consortium and Rosalie Ber, Elizabeth Brondolo, William Byham, Kate Cannon, Diane Fassil, Colette Frayne, Victoria Gutherie, Hank Jonas, Daniela Kramer, Gary Latham, Cindy McCauley, Jeff Monroy, Michael Moore, and David Peterson. These people are the real heroes in the field, because they have shown the rest of us how to apply emotional intelligence in making workers and workplaces more productive.

Our research assistants at Rutgers University—Cornelia Roche, Rob Emmerling, and Kim Cowan—helped with library research, identification of the model programs, and the logistics of running the consortium smoothly. We also thank our families for their warmth, love, and support.

Cary Cherniss
Mitchel Adler
May 2000

EI

Emotional Intelligence— Building a Business Case

Emotional intelligence (EI) can be defined in many ways, but on the most basic level it is the ability to accurately identify and understand one's own emotional reactions and those of others. It also involves the ability to regulate one's emotions, to use them to make good decisions, and to act effectively (Mayer, Salovey, and Caruso 1998). Emotional intelligence is the basis for personal qualities such as realistic self-confidence, personal integrity, knowledge of personal strengths and weaknesses, resilience in times of change or adversity, self-motivation, perseverance, and the knack for getting along well with others.

The Tylenol Crisis

According to Peter Dinella (1999) of Johnson & Johnson (J&J), "The Tylenol tragedy was without precedent in the history of corporate crises. In the fall of 1982, an unknown criminal poisoned pain-relief capsules with cyanide, and seven people in the Chicago area died. Overnight, Tylenol toppled from its preeminent position as the nation's leading analgesic product. Many experts predicted that it would never recover. By early 1983, five months after the tragedy, Tylenol recaptured nearly 70 percent of the market it previously held."

Dinella goes on: "In thinking about how the Tylenol poisonings were handled, I see many related factors all helping to resolve the crisis. Certainly having a credo, a statement of our values and responsibilities, was a dominant factor. It provided guidance and constantly tested all J&J managers as they agonized through the many decisions that were made. Leadership was another dominant factor. This was untested water; companies never had this type of situation to deal with before. Much was at stake: the trust of our customers and the incredible demands to build and return shareholder value."

Dinella continues, "James E. Burke was our chairman at the time. Case studies have described in detail the business impact on J&J of the Tylenol poisonings. Details about media coverage, marketing decisions, competition, and advertising approaches dominate those case studies. Some even bring in the business-ethics aspect of the situation. However, none to date, have really connected the issue of emotional intelligence and leadership. What strikes me now, however, is the high level of emotional intelligence Jim Burke possessed. The following hallmarks of emotional intelligence were in abundant supply: self-confidence; trustworthiness and integrity; comfort with ambiguity; openness to change; strong drive to achieve; optimism, even in the face of failure; organizational commitment; service to clients and customers; effectiveness in leading change; persuasiveness; and expertise building and leading teams."

Dinella provides this example of Burke's emotional intelligence in handling the Tylenol crisis: "When we got back into the marketplace with tamper-resistant, safety-sealed packages, there was a lot of pressure early on to get back into television advertising. It was the view of some that advertising would help reassure fearful consumers that the new packaging was safe. Burke, on the other hand, argued that advertising would have the opposite effect: 'There's nothing more offensive to me, if I'm frightened, than somebody telling me I ought to buy their product, and I know I ought to buy it…but I can't.' Burke's view prevailed."

On the other hand, EI does not just mean being nice, because there are times when effective action calls for being firm and tough. Emotional intelligence also does not mean giving free rein to feelings, because effective action sometimes requires personal restraint and self-control. Emotional intelligence is not fixed genetically or set in early childhood. In fact, people seem to develop greater EI throughout most of the adult years; other things being equal, 40- and 50-year-olds tend to be more emotionally intelligent than 20-year-olds (Bar-On 1997).

Using Emotional Intelligence to Survive a Kidnapping

In November 1981, Brigadier General James L. Dozier of the U.S. Army was kidnapped by the Red Brigades, a notorious Italian terrorist group. Dozier had no contact with the outside world for three months until he finally was located and freed. In a letter that he later wrote about the experience, he revealed how EI helped save his life (Campbell 1990).

He described how he became aware of how anxious and excited his captors were becoming as a result of the media furor over the kidnapping. As he put it, "They were bouncing off the walls with anxiety." He realized that this excited anxiety could be dangerous for him, which could have heightened his own anxiety. Nevertheless, he kept his own anxiety under control, and he remembered learning in a leadership training program that modeling could be a powerful means for influencing other people's actions and emotions. So, he set out to make himself as calm and quiet as possible. Just as he had hoped, his own calm spread to his captors. They also calmed down, and Dozier was convinced that this saved his life. In this situation, Dozier's ability to become aware of the emotional dynamics and their likely consequences, his skill in maintaining control over his own emotions and impulses, and his ability to influence the emotional reactions of his captors helped save his life.

Emotional intelligence is not really new. What is new is that now, more than ever, data is available about what matters for successful action at work. Recent advances in brain science provide better understanding of the role that emotion plays in effective thought and action. More information is available about how emotional, social, and cognitive parts of the brain work together and what can happen when these parts of the brain are out of synchrony.

Emotional intelligence matters more than ever. Personal qualities, such as resilience, optimism, and initiative, have become more important in recent years due to the massive changes occurring in the American and global workplace. Technical innovation, global competition, and pressures of institutional investors are just three of the factors contributing to this turbulence. For instance, consider the effect of technical innovation. Prior to about 1980, the pace of technical change in the office environment was glacial compared to what it is today. A clerk typist who learned how to type in 1960 on an electric typewriter could walk into an office in 1980 and immediately operate the typewriters. Since the advent of word processors and the subsequent improvements in word-processing programs, typists must upgrade their technical skills every three to five years to keep up with the myriad of competing programs that use different commands. Coping with this pace of change requires patience, self-discipline, and flexibility.

Another significant result of this rapid change has been the downsizing of the organization. As organizations shrink, people who remain are more accountable and more visible. They must interact with more peers, more subordinates, and more customers. They must become more adept at handling not only relationships but also feelings—their own and others'. In short, EI was never more important for American workers and their employers.

Although many people now appreciate the importance of EI for individual and organizational effectiveness, such was not always the case. For many decades during the early part of this century, most people assumed that it was cognitive ability, as measured by the intelligence quotient (IQ) test, the Scholastic Aptitude Test (SAT), or the Graduate Management Admission Test (GMAT), that counted. Beginning in the 1970s, a growing body of research showed that purely cognitive ability, while important, does not represent the whole picture. In fact, IQ accounts for at most 25 percent of the variance in individual success. In many studies, it accounts for as little as 4 percent. Technical expertise adds to this, but even cognitive ability and technical expertise leave much to be explained. Thousands of very bright, technically able individuals fail to reach their potential because they lack sufficient EI.

Emotional intelligence and cognitive ability actually work together for effective action in organizations. Without EI, cognitive abilities suffer. For instance, when one becomes upset, the ability to process information and make decisions diminishes. Effective communication, which involves cognitive ability, also depends on emotional capacities, such as being able to gauge an audience's reactions and present information in a way that has emotional impact.

Therefore, it is not surprising that numerous studies point to EI as critical for success at work. Goleman (1998) reviewed the competence models for 181 positions taken from 121 companies and found that two-thirds of the abilities essential for effective performance were emotional competencies. For leadership positions, the proportion rose to nearly 90 percent. In other words, at the highest levels of an organization, the difference between superior performance and average performance depends almost completely on EI.

This is not to say that technical skill and cognitive abilities are unimportant. Managers, executives, and professionals require a certain level of these abilities—threshold competencies—just to get in the door. Once an individual becomes an executive or manager, what distinguishes that person's performance from another's are self-confidence, self-control, and the ability to motivate others. In other words, having an IQ of 130 instead of 120 will not make that much difference for a manager but having a bit more self-confidence or being a little more skilled in handling one's own feelings and those of others can make a big difference.

This point was particularly well illustrated with research conducted at a large beverage and food company by the consulting firm Hay/McBer (McClelland 1998). They developed a competence model for executives that included such EI-based competencies as initiative and achievement drive, influence and team leadership, empathy, self-confidence, and organizational awareness. All told, there were 12 competencies in the model, 10 of which were aspects of EI. They then identified a group of division heads who reached a critical level on six of the 12 competencies representing the entire spectrum of EI, and their performance was compared to those who lacked them. The results were impressive: Division heads who possessed the competencies outperformed their targets by 15 to 20 percent, while those who lacked them underperformed by almost 20 percent (McClelland 1998).

This same general pattern has emerged in other competency studies involving other types of jobs. For instance, at a national insurance company, insurance sales agents who were very strong in at least five of eight key competencies, including self-confidence, initiative, and empathy, sold policies with an average premium of $114,000. Those who were weak in these competencies sold policies worth only $54,000 on average.

While some studies have shown how a high level of EI is linked to superior performance, other studies document what happens when people lack these competencies. The Center for Creative Leadership studied executives who had derailed and found that the problem was never a deficit in cognitive ability. The two most common traits of those who failed were rigidity and poor relationships (Leslie and van Velsor 1996).

This growing body of research, along with a wealth of personal experience, has led employers to change their ideas about what is most important in an employee. No longer do they emphasize technical skills and raw intelligence alone. Employers increasingly recognize that, given sufficient cognitive ability and technical skills to hold the job, social and emotional competencies matter most. For instance, a national survey conducted by the Department of Labor and the American Society for Training & Development (ASTD) to elucidate characteristics sought by employers in entry-level workers found that the most important qualities were personal management (self-esteem, goal setting and motivation, personal and career development), interpersonal skills (negotiation and teamwork), and organizational effectiveness and leadership (Carnevale, Gainer, and Meltzer 1988).

Employers also value these competencies for entry-level management positions. In a study of which characteristics are desired by corporations in job candidates holding master's of business administration degrees, the three most desirable capabilities were found to be communications skills, interpersonal skills, and initiative (Dowd and Liedtka 1994).

Unfortunately, what employers want does not appear to be what they get. Another survey of American employers found that more than half the people who work for them lack the motivation to continue learning and improving on the job. Four of 10 are not able to work cooperatively with fellow employees, and just 19 percent of those applying for entry-level jobs have enough self-discipline in their work habits (Harris Education Research Council 1991).

Even more alarming is the research suggesting that the next generation of workers will be weaker still in EI. Parents and teachers of 7- to 16-year-olds were surveyed in the mid-1970s and asked to evaluate their children. A similar sample was studied in the late 1980s. The results indicate that on every indicator of EI, the children had become worse (Achenbach and Howell 1989). They were significantly more withdrawn and more likely to have social problems, and they were more likely to have attention or thinking problems. Delinquency, aggression, anxiety, and depression also increased. What this data means is that the generation of workers now entering the American workplace is less likely than previous generations to possess the social and emotional qualities that are essential for effective performance.

This trend represents a major challenge for employers and for HR professionals in particular. It is no wonder that HR personnel increasingly are being called upon to provide training—not just in technical skills—but also in social and emotional competencies that are essential for success. In the next chapter these competencies and their links to EI are described.

2

EI

Emotional Competencies
That Lead to Success

Emotional intelligence, on the most basic level, is the ability to accurately identify and understand one's own emotional reactions and those of others. This is the most fundamental definition, but it can be misleading in two ways. First, it would be more accurate to speak of emotional "intelligences," because EI is not a single ability. Second, EI by itself does not lead to the sort of outstanding performance referred to in chapter 1. Success actually depends on a set of emotional and social competencies that build on EI, in the same way that specific cognitive abilities may be linked to general intelligence as measured by the IQ test.

For example, a basic dimension of EI is social awareness—the ability to identify and understand the emotional reactions of others. People who are strong in this dimension are able to develop easily a specific competency such as "service orientation." That competency contributes to superior performance in many occupations. Nevertheless, the underlying EI of social awareness in itself does not contribute to superior performance to the extent that a strong service orientation does.

The term *emotional competency* is used in a specific way in this book: It refers to a learned ability, based on EI, that improves job performance. Emotional competencies can include attitudes and beliefs, as exemplified by achievement drive and self-confidence, as well as skills and abilities. Emotional competencies, however, are learned; they are not innate. People are not born with a high degree of self-confidence or achievement drive.

Based on his review of nearly 200 different competency models, Goleman (1998) identified 25 social and emotional competencies that most strongly predict superior performance in many occupations. He organized these competencies into the five dimensions of EI (Goleman 1995): self-awareness, self-regulation, self-motivation, social awareness, and social skills. Recent research using the emotional competence inventory, a measure of EI developed by Boyatzis, Goleman, and Rhee (in press), led to a refined version of the original model. This generic competency framework consists of four dimensions and 19 emotional competencies (table 2-1), which were distilled in large part from a handful of studies (U.S. Office of Personnel Management 1996; Spencer and Spencer 1993; Rosier and Jeffrey 1994, 1995).

Goleman proposed that the four broad dimensions of EI—self-awareness, self-management, social awareness, and social

Table 2-1. The four dimensions and 19 competencies associated with emotional intelligence.[1]

DIMENSION 1: SELF-AWARENESS

Knowing one's internal states, preferences, resources, and intuitions

1. Emotional self-awareness: Recognizing one's emotions and their effects
2. Accurate self-assessment: Knowing one's strengths and limits
3. Self-confidence: A strong sense of one's self-worth and capabilities

DIMENSION 2: SELF-MANAGEMENT

Managing one's internal states, impulses, and resources to facilitate reaching goals

4. Adaptability: Flexibility in handling change
5. Self-control: Keeping disruptive emotions and impulses in check

[1] The material in this table was drawn in part from Goleman (1998).

Table 2-1. The four dimensions and 19 competencies associated with emotional intelligence. *(continued)*

6. Conscientiousness and reliability: Taking responsibility for personal performance; maintaining standards of honesty and integrity
7. Initiative and innovation: Readiness to act on opportunities; being comfortable with novel ideas, approaches, and new information
8. Achievement drive: Striving to improve or meet a standard of excellence; persistence in pursuing goals despite obstacles and setbacks

DIMENSION 3: SOCIAL AWARENESS

Awareness of others' feelings, needs, and concerns

9. Empathy: Sensing others' feelings and perspectives and taking an active interest in their concerns
10. Service orientation: Anticipating, recognizing, and meeting customers' needs
11. Organizational awareness: Reading a group's emotional currents and power relationships
12. Developing others: Sensing others' developmental needs and bolstering their abilities

DIMENSION 4: SOCIAL SKILLS

Adeptness at inducing desirable responses in others

13. Leadership: Inspiring and guiding individuals and groups; aligning with the goals of the group or organization
14. Influence: Wielding effective tactics for persuasion
15. Change catalyst: Initiating or managing change
16. Communication: Listening openly and sending convincing messages
17. Conflict management: Negotiating and resolving disagreements
18. Collaboration and building bonds: Working with others toward shared goals; nurturing instrumental relationships
19. Team capabilities: Creating group synergy in pursuing collective goals

SOURCE: Reprinted with permission of Daniel Goleman, 2000.

skills—are interdependent and, to some degree, hierarchical. To understand what Goleman means by this, take the example of Martin, a flight attendant who was confronted with an angry passenger. To deal effectively with the situation, Martin first needed to be aware of his own emotional reaction, because the passenger's behavior could cause Martin to experience emotions ranging from apprehension to annoyance. If Martin were unaware of his own emotional reaction, it could interfere with his taking effective action. Awareness, though, is rarely enough; Martin also had to control his emotional response. By calming himself, he was ultimately able to help the passenger calm down. Once Martin became calm, he could tune in to the passenger. What was it that upset the passenger?

By understanding the passenger's feelings and the reasons behind the feelings, Martin was able to take action: He offered to hold the fussy infant squirming on the passenger's lap, and he did so in a way that did not make the passenger more embarrassed or angry. In this situation, Martin used competencies associated with each of the four dimensions of EI. Although it happened very quickly and without conscious awareness, Martin's self-awareness made self-management possible, and self-management made empathy possible, and all three of these abilities made it easier for the attendant to use effective social skills.

This example also points to another important aspect of the model: A high degree of competence in just one of the four dimensions of EI usually is not enough to achieve superior performance. A recent series of studies reported by McClelland (1998) suggests that to be a star, one needs a sufficiently high level of about six different competencies spread across all four areas. It is not enough to excel in self-awareness or self-management or even social skills. The research also suggests that the competencies needed for success differ with the nature of the job. They also depend on one's level in the organization and the organization's culture and strategic focus. For instance, achievement drive usually is a strong predictor of success among executives, but in very mechanistic, bureaucratic organizations, too much achievement drive can be a liability. Entrepreneurial individuals with a strong need for achievement most likely will not be sufficiently rewarded, and they will be frustrated in such a work setting. Although the most critical competencies vary by job and organization, stars typically are distinguished from average performers by half a dozen or so emotional competencies spread across all four dimensions.

DIMENSION 1: SELF-AWARENESS

Self-awareness is the core of EI. Three critical competencies are linked to it (table 2-1). The first is emotional self-awareness, the ability to know which emotions are being experienced and why. People with a high degree of this competency also realize how their feelings affect what they think, do, and say; they are clear about their values and goals.

This first competency may seem "soft," but it actually is essential for success in business and the professions, and most workers use it every day. Consider all of the decisions that rely on a certain amount of intuition or gut feelings in addition to objective facts. Credit managers, for example, have to use more than just the numbers in deciding whether to approve a deal. Executives must decide whether to invest the money and time necessary to develop a new product. Managers must decide which applicant for a job will fit best on a team.

Several studies suggest that the most successful performers know how to use their feelings in making such decisions. A study of 60 highly successful entrepreneurs (Ehringer 1995) found that all but one went beyond simply gathering the relevant information to weigh it against intuition or gut feeling in making important decisions. Similar results came from a study (Agor 1986) of 3,000 executives in a wide range of fields. Those at the top were particularly adept at using intuition in reaching decisions. As one put it, "Sometimes the brain says, 'Well, that's going to make a lot of people ticked off,' or whatever, and yet this sixth sense says, 'Yeah, but it feels right.' And I have learned to trust that." Another successful entrepreneur said, "It's like your gut tells you things and there's a chemical reaction that's going on in your body, which is triggered by your mind, and tightening your stomach muscles, so your gut is saying, 'This doesn't feel right'" (Goleman 1998).

Emotional awareness contributes to better performance in at least one other way: It helps people to align better their values and actions. When actions and values are not in alignment, when actions are not congruent with what is best for the self or others, it is like driving with the emergency brake on. Perhaps the driver is not aware that it is causing drag and sapping energy, especially as life speeds along, and the driver is too busy to notice. Eventually, it can lead to burnout and failure. When individuals are able to engage in work that fits their values, it releases an enormous amount of energy. These people are the lucky ones who have a passion about their work and who usually excel at it. For instance, in a study of hundreds of knowledge workers, Kelley (1998) found that the superior performers knew intuitively what they did best and enjoyed, and they made choices based on that understanding.

A second competency associated with self-awareness is *accurate self-assessment*. People who are strong in this quality are aware of their strengths and weaknesses. They also tend to be reflective and eager to learn from experience. Perhaps most important, they are open to candid feedback. Superior performance requires that people first are aware of their strengths and weaknesses so that they can work in ways that exploit the former and avoid the latter. It also requires that people work on improving themselves, and that continuous improvement is a personal and corporate

The Manager Who Lacked Emotional Awareness

Bill was a brilliant, highly motivated performer who had risen steadily in his profession. He had, however, at least one major flaw: an awful temper. He would quickly become impatient with those who did not meet his standards. Nobody wanted to work with him.

During one staff meeting, Bill became particularly impatient with two employees who were making a presentation. His face became red, the veins on his neck bulged, and his speech became nearly incoherent as he expressed his anger. No one said anything about it at the time, but the next day one of his peers, who had been at the meeting and witnessed what had occurred, went into Bill's office to see how he was feeling about the incident. The colleague asked Bill if he still was angry about what had happened at the meeting the day before, and Bill quizzically looked back at him. "Angry?" he asked with bemusement. "What do you mean? I wasn't angry about anything at the meeting."

It is possible that Bill was trying to avoid responsibility for his behavior, but his genuine puzzlement suggested that he simply was not aware of his own emotional reactions and their effect on his behavior. It became clear that lack of emotional awareness was an important factor in Bill's difficulty with people.

priority. The beginning of successful self-improvement is an awareness of where improvement is needed.

Not surprisingly, managers who get into trouble, who alienate their peers and employees, and who are most likely to derail, tend to be the last to realize that they have fatal flaws. A comparison of executives who derailed and those who did well found that both groups had weaknesses, but those who succeeded learned from their mistakes and shortcomings (McCall and Lombardo 1983). Similarly, a study of several hundred managers from 12 different organizations found that accurate self-assessment was associated with superior performance (Boyatzis 1982). This key competency also was found in every star performer identified in a study of several hundred knowledge workers (Kelley 1998).

The Misfit Attorney

Margaret Williams had many sterling qualities, but accurate self-assessment was not one of them. This weakness proved to be very costly for her. Margaret had been a brilliant student all of her life. She went to an elite college where she majored and excelled in philosophy. As graduation approached, she considered going to graduate school and embarking on an academic career, but she was a committed and passionate social activist. She wanted to do something more "relevant" than teach and write books about philosophy, so she went to law school instead. She was admitted to one of the most prestigious schools, and she easily made law review. When she graduated, she had the opportunity to clerk for judges or to work in a large law firm. She decided, however, to go to work for the local legal-aid society instead.

Within two months, Margaret came to hate her work. She had never been so bored or frustrated. She spent most of her time on the telephone finding out why her clients' utilities had been turned off or why their welfare checks were late. She complained that a well-trained clerk with a high school education could do what she did most of the time.

Margaret thought seriously of changing jobs, but she kept putting off the decision to do so. Gradually, she became too comfortable to change, even though she still was unhappy and unfulfilled in her work. Finally, after spending five years with the legal-aid society, Margaret began to look for other jobs. Unfortunately, she discovered that after working in legal aid for so long, the only jobs she could get were in that area of the law.

Margaret decided to change careers. She began studying urban planning part-time, and after a few years she earned her master's degree. She found a job in the city's planning department and finally left the legal-aid society. She was happier now but still not very stimulated or fulfilled in her work.

Nevertheless, she stayed on for three years. Then came a budget crisis and with it, the elimination of her job. Desperate over the impending loss of benefits, Margaret pleaded for some other job in city government. Because she had a law degree, she was given a position in the legal department.

Margaret was not happy to be back in law. She spent the first few weeks doing little or nothing, but then she found some bankruptcy cases that no one was pursuing. She discovered that with a little effort, she could recapture hundreds of thousands of dollars that the city was owed. She also found that the area of municipal bankruptcy law was an area with many interesting intellectual problems still to be solved. She began to work on big cases that actually helped change the law in this area.

Margaret came to be recognized as one of the leading practitioners in her field. And for the first time in 12 years, she was intellectually challenged and fulfilled in her work.

As Margaret looked back over her career, she realized that she had made some big mistakes. She never had recognized how important it was for her to be intellectually challenged in her work. She now saw that in some ways all those years had been a waste. If she had known herself better, she would have found fulfilling work much sooner, and her life would have been inestimably more satisfying.

The third competency associated with self-awareness is *self-confidence.* Self-confident people are more effective, because they present themselves with self-assurance. They have a certain presence, a charisma that inspires and motivates others. They also can voice views that are unpopular. They are willing to go out on a limb for what is right. They are decisive, able to make sound decisions even in the face of uncertainty or pressure.

A number of studies have found that self-confidence is associated with superior performance. For instance, among 112 entry-level accountants, those with the strongest self-efficacy (a belief that one has the ability to succeed) were rated highest on job performance by supervisors 10 months later. Self-efficacy was a stronger predictor of performance than the actual level of skill or training that one had before being hired (Saks 1995). Also, landmark studies of managerial success at AT&T showed that self-confidence early in a career predicted later career success (Howard and Bray 1988). These results are not just limited to AT&T. Boyatzis (1982) also found that self-confidence was linked to superior performance of managers who had worked in 12 different companies.

DIMENSION 2: SELF-MANAGEMENT

The self-management competencies (table 2-1) affect one's ability to handle stress, manage anger, control impulses, and remain motivated even in the face of setbacks. Self-control is the first and most basic of the self-management competencies. People with this competency are able to manage their impulsive feelings and distressing emotions well, stay composed and positive even in difficult situations, and think clearly under pressure. It is well known that excessive stress can lead to a variety of physical symptoms, and worker illness increasingly is a bottom-line issue for American employers. Stress can affect the bottom line in other ways, too. People who are unable to handle stress well find it difficult to concentrate. Memory and decision making also are adversely affected by stress. Therefore, it is not surprising that among store managers in a retail chain, the most successful, as measured by net profit, sales per square foot, and sales per employee, were the ones who were best able to handle stress (Lusch and Serpkenci 1990). In certain occupations, the ability to remain calm in tense situations can be even more important. New York traffic agents who responded calmly when faced with angry motorists had the fewest incidents escalate into violence (Brondolo et al. 1996).

The CEO Who Could Not Take the Heat

He was a new CEO who still was in his honeymoon period. He was popular among many different groups within the organization. Notwithstanding, one group of employees was unhappy about certain policies in the organization. At a meeting with shareholders, the group chose to make their views known by standing during a presentation by the CEO and challenging him to do something about the policies.

The CEO was visibly shaken. Rather than engage the employees in a way that might diffuse the situation and help restore order, he gathered up his notes and made a hasty exit. From then on, he avoided any situation in which he might encounter conflict and confrontation. Soon, he developed a reputation for being aloof and insensitive to the concerns of employees. His closest associates denied that this was the case; they found him personable and open. Beyond his closest and most trusted subordinates, however, he seemed stiff and awkward. His anxiety—or more accurately, his inability to manage his anxiety constructively—became a major liability for him and for his organization.

Effective self-control does not mean suppressing emotion. People with this competency are able to use their emotions effectively, and sometimes that means expressing emotion. In fact, the study of New York traffic agents found that the agents who tried to suppress their anger were less productive than were those who expressed it constructively. Another study of nearly 2,000 supervisors, managers, and executives in American companies found that those who were more spontaneous actually performed better, not worse (Boyatzis 1982).

One emotion that is particularly helpful for superior performance is flow, a state that accompanies intense absorption in an interesting, optimally challenging task. People enjoy their work most and work most efficiently when they are in flow. Whether it results from climbing a mountain or closing a big deal, flow helps people work better. Although work is an important source of flow, and people seem to be in a state of flow about half the time at work on average, this percentage varies greatly among individuals (LeFevre 1988). Those who are able to find ways to increase the amount of time that they spend in flow at work tend to be the stars. Self-control, along with acute emotional self-awareness, is the competency they use to achieve a state of flow so frequently.

Closely related to self-control is *adaptability.* People with this competency are flexible, and they handle change well. They are not thrown by shifting priorities; in fact, rather than being uncomfortable with change, they enjoy it. They are comfortable with ambiguity and remain calm in the face of the unexpected.

In the new world of work, adaptability is a particularly valuable competency. People no longer can assume that their jobs will be secure indefinitely. Even careers change. For example, those who went into medicine 20 years ago or even 10 years ago now find themselves in a very different profession because of the tumultuous transformation brought about by managed care. The most successful and satisfied physicians are those who have adapted to these changes. The same is true for many other professions.

Even if one's profession is not changing rapidly, chances are that one's organization is. The pace of change in organizations has become dizzying. It is not uncommon for people to have a different job with a different manager and a different team every year or two. Those who can ride the turbulent waves of change that sweep over the American workplace will be the superior performers. Those who cannot adapt will find themselves at a disadvantage.

The third self-management competency is *conscientiousness*. Those with this competency meet commitments and keep promises. They are organized and careful about their work. They do the right thing even when it is unpopular. They are punctual, self-disciplined, and helpful to those with whom they work. Conscientious workers are so valued that their performance ratings often are higher than they would be if based purely on objective performance. Conscientiousness also pays off directly in terms of better performance. For example, among sales representatives for a major appliance firm, those who were most conscientious had the highest volume of sales (Barrick, Mount, and Strauss 1993).

The Supervisor Who Could

At the age of 25, Susan was one of the youngest supervisors in the state agency where she worked. She also had one of the toughest employees to supervise—her secretary, Selma. Selma had been working in state government for over 20 years. During that time, she had always received satisfactory performance reviews. It was widely recognized, however, that Selma's performance was far from satisfactory, and it had been that way for some time. Selma's previous supervisors had never bothered to discipline her or insist on higher standards, because they believed that it was futile to do so in a state system governed by stringent civil service laws. As a result, Selma's performance steadily declined.

Susan had been warned about Selma before she even got the promotion. "It's just too hard to fire someone who is covered by civil service," she was told, "especially when they have received satisfactory reviews for so long." Susan was conscientious, though. When she saw how little Selma did and the adverse consequences on her staff's performance, she decided that she had to do something even if it meant taking on the whole civil service system.

Susan met with Selma and calmly told her that her performance was not acceptable. She sat quietly while Selma made excuses, and then she told Selma that her performance would have to improve. Two weeks later, after there had been no discernible improvement, Susan again met with Selma and told her that she would have to write Selma up for her many lapses and inadequacies. This time Selma did not bother making excuses. Instead she yelled, threatened, and stormed out of the office.

This pattern continued for the next four months. It took an enormous amount of self-control on Susan's part. She dreaded having to meet with Selma, but she never lost her composure and she never gave up. Susan received much sympathy and more than a little admiration from her co-workers, but no one gave her much support. Nevertheless, Susan persisted, even when Selma complained that Susan's "harassment" had made her ill, and she threatened a lawsuit against Susan and the state. As Selma's sick days mounted, Susan calmly informed her that this constituted one more way in which her performance was adversely affecting the division.

Susan knew that even with Selma's previous record and the protection provided to employees by the civil service system, she could eventually terminate Selma with enough documentation. Susan was determined to terminate Selma, no matter how long it took. After four months, though, Selma finally gave up and agreed to retire. Susan's effort in this trying situation demonstrated how valuable self-control and conscientiousness are in supervising difficult employees.

Too much conscientiousness by itself, however, can lead to trouble. Conscientious people often expect much not only of themselves but of others, as well. They can become impatient and overly critical. Their tendency to disapprove of even the slightest transgression can alienate those around them. Also, conscientious individuals may be so intent on following the rules and doing the right thing that creativity suffers. Therefore, conscientiousness works best when it is linked to empathy, social skill, and another competency—initiative and innovation.

People with *initiative and innovation* seek out new ideas from a variety of sources, entertain original solutions to problems, generate new ideas, and adopt fresh perspectives in their thinking. They are ready to seize opportunities when they come along, pursue goals beyond what is required or expected, cut through red tape, and bend the rules when necessary to get the job done. This competency can pay off for organizations at any level. For example, a shipping clerk realized that his company did enough business with a particular overnight shipper to get a discount and receive a computer to track shipping orders. He took the initiative and approached the CEO to present the idea. The company adopted the change and saved $30,000 a year (Spencer and Spencer 1993).

Initiative is useful in many occupations. Managers with initiative anticipate problems before they occur and take corrective action. Salespersons with initiative seek opportunities and act on them, such as the trust officer, who, when he was in the hospital with a serious illness, sold an account to his doctor (Goleman 1998).

Those with initiative also tend to persist in seeking goals despite obstacles and setbacks. They are optimists. When they experience a failure, they are more likely to take stock and try to learn from it, then move on with their lives. Pessimists, on the other hand, are more likely to see the failure as caused by a personal flaw or an external factor over which they have no control.

They tend to give up rather than persist. Persistence can be useful in many different occupations, but especially in sales. At Met Life, for example, optimists sold 29 percent more life insurance during their first year than did pessimists, and the second year they sold 130 percent more (Schulman 1995).

Initiative, as is the case for conscientiousness, must be tempered with self-control and social awareness. Managers who are high in initiative but low in self-control and social awareness may run roughshod over those with whom they work. They are the ones who tend to micromanage and ignore people's feelings in their urgency to take action (Goleman 1998).

The last self-management competency is *achievement drive.* People with this competency are result-oriented. They set challenging goals and strive to meet them. They constantly look for ways to do better. They take calculated risks. Among executives, achievement drive is the competency that most strongly distinguishes stars from the rest of the pack.

People with strong achievement drive are especially eager for feedback, because feedback is how they measure themselves and discover ways to improve. For this reason, successful entrepreneurs often say that money is less important for what it can buy than as a measure of how well they are doing. In addition to seeking feedback, people with a strong need to achieve also seek out information. They are constantly scanning their environment in pursuit of ideas that can help them to perform even better.

DIMENSION 3: SOCIAL AWARENESS

The third dimension of the framework—social awareness—embraces four EI competencies (table 2-1). The most basic of these competencies is empathy. People with this competency are attentive to the emotional cues of others and listen well. They also take an active interest in others' concerns. The essence of empathy is the ability to detect what others are feeling even if those feelings go unexpressed verbally. People often do not speak of their feelings especially in the workplace where there often are norms against doing so. Nevertheless, smooth social interaction requires that people be able to understand what others are feeling. Empathic individuals can figure out what people are feeling through their tone of voice, facial expression, and body language.

Empathy is important in any job involving people. In the sales profession, it is crucial. A survey of retail buyers, for example, found that apparel sales representatives who were perceived to be empathic were favored over those who were affable and outgoing (Pilling and Eroglu 1994). Research in medical care has found that physicians who lack empathy get sued more often (Levinson et al. 1997).

Empathy also is valuable for all leaders. The most effective leaders are those who can discern the feelings of their followers. They have a special connection with those whom they lead, and they use this to touch them in a way that inspires commitment and dedication. Empathic leaders are especially valuable when times are tough. Employees who remain after a downsizing, for example, will regain their morale and commitment more quickly when their bosses understand and sympathize with what they are experiencing.

An Empathic Manager

Paula was one of the most effective customer service workers in Jane's group, but one day a major customer complained to Jane about the way that Paula had handled an order. Jane was concerned about losing the goodwill of one of the firm's most important customers, but she realized that if Paula had made a mistake, she already must feel bad about it. So she arranged to go out to lunch with Paula, and after a few minutes of savoring good food in a good restaurant, she raised the delicate subject of the irate customer. She did so by assuring Paula that she knew that this customer could be difficult and demanding and that she also knew that Paula must feel pretty bad about the whole situation. Then she just listened as Paula told her side of the story. As Jane expected, the customer had been somewhat unreasonable, but, because she felt safe and supported, Paula also was able to see her contribution to the problem and took some responsibility for what happened. Jane recognized that Paula now knew what she needed to do to make the situation right, and so she refrained from offering any specific advice.

Because she received empathic support from her boss, Paula remained with the company for many years, turning down more lucrative offers from other companies. Eventually, Paula became a manager herself, and she tried to model her own approach on Jane's. Doing so helped her to become the top manager in the company.

Empathy also is the competency most strongly linked to tolerance for diversity. People who score high in empathy respect and relate well to people from varied backgrounds, and they are more likely to understand diverse world views. Highly empathic individuals also are likely to see diversity as a strength. Empathy allows one to view the world through others' eyes, and this view helps reduce the influence of stereotypes and prejudice. Empathic leaders are better able to understand and appreciate the unique contributions of every individual; this appreciation allows them to leverage the benefits that a more diverse workforce can offer a business.

Those who lack empathy are more likely to respond to people who are different from themselves on the basis of simplistic stereotypes. Relationships based on stereotypes rather than empathy are likely to interfere with both individual and group performance.

Empathy should not be confused with psychologizing or agreeing. Those who respond to our expressions of feeling with a comment about its psychological roots or another type of interpretation are not empathizing; they are psychologizing (Goleman 1998). On the other hand, empathy does not require agreeing with other people, only an understanding of their perspectives on a situation. For example, top negotiators are very good at empathizing with the other party in a conflict, and they use this ability to find the best ways of meeting everyone's needs. Their empathic ability leads to win-win outcomes; they do not give away the store (Goleman 1998).

Closely related to empathy is the competency of *service orientation*. People with this competency are good at anticipating, recognizing, and meeting customers' needs. They seek ways to increase customers' satisfaction and loyalty. They are likely to become not only an advisor but also an advocate for the customer. Such people build strong loyalty among those they serve. That phenomenon makes people with this competency particularly valuable, for, as Drucker (1995) noted, the purpose of business is not to make a sale but to make and keep a customer.

Service orientation is especially important in jobs that involve sales and customer service; more and more jobs are now involving such services. In the modern organization, everyone from the secretary and maintenance worker, to the computer programmer and business office manager, right up to the CEO has customers. Service has become the dominant theme in American business, and this fact has helped to fuel the biggest peacetime expansion of the economy in our history. Given this context, those who excel in service orientation are likely to be especially valued in any organization.

Another competency closely linked to empathy is *developing others*. In the learning organization that has become the ideal in today's workplace, personal development is a core function. Everyone needs to be learning and growing constantly. People who are good at developing others are the ones who seek out opportunities to help subordinates, peers, and even their bosses to learn and grow. They are skilled at sensing what other people's developmental needs are, and they are adept at providing coaching, mentoring, and feedback in ways that help people to meet these needs. As bosses, they are also effective in providing people with assignments that help them develop new skills.

Developing others is an especially important competency for those who supervise frontline workers. For sales managers, this competency is the one most frequently found among the very top performers (Spencer and Spencer 1993). For sales managers, it is not their ability to sell but their ability to help others sell that is the cornerstone of their success. The same is true for most other first-level supervisors: Those who are effective in developing others not only help employees perform better, they also enhance job satisfaction and loyalty.

Developing others involves both attitudes and skills. Those who are strong in this competency have a strong personal interest in helping others, especially those with whom they work. They also appreciate and understand others especially well. This allows them to sense what others need and to develop strong, positive relationships, which are important for personal development. In addition, those who excel in developing others are skillful in providing feedback. They are able to give both positive and negative feedback in ways that inspire others to do better.

As with many of the other competencies, too much emphasis on developing others can become counterproductive in certain situations. Coaching and developing others is an important part of a manager's job, but it is only one part. Managers often must weigh the developmental needs of their employees against the needs of the organization. Supervisors and managers who devote too much time to coaching and too little to leading are not likely to be superior performers (Boyatzis 1982).

One other important competency associated with social awareness is *organizational awareness.* People with this competency are able to accurately read power relationships and detect crucial social networks. They understand the social forces that shape the views and actions of their clients, customers, and competitors. This ability allows them to avoid many pitfalls and to manage conflicts effectively. It also enables them to wield more influence than those who are oblivious to how things are done in an organization.

Every organization has both a formal and informal structure. Every executive vice president, for example, has a certain amount of power, and in the formal structure they are supposed to be equal in this respect. Some vice presidents, however, are "more equal" than others. Those within and without the organization will be more successful if they are aware of these differences in power and how they affect the life of the organization.

Knowing where the power centers are and how decisions get made is only part of organizational awareness. Equally important is being aware of and respecting the underlying norms and values that make up the organization's culture. Some people seem to be oblivious to the culture of the organization in which they work, even after spending years in that setting. Such individuals tend to find it difficult to succeed beyond a certain point, no matter how great their technical skill and ability. On the other hand, those who understand how things are done tend to excel.

An Organizationally Aware Manager

Martin had just been picked to head up a new division in a large pharmaceutical company. He had waited a long time for this promotion, and he relished having some autonomy. The CEO assured him that he would have free rein to do whatever he wanted provided that he meet his productivity goals.

Martin realized, however, that the CEO had a lot at stake in this new venture and so would be anxious to know how things were going. He also found that the vice president for finance liked to receive detailed financial data on each division every month even though it was not officially required. Therefore, even though no one told him to do so, Martin sent regular reports to the CEO, summarizing what he had done and his plans for the immediate future. He also arranged to have financial data sent to the vice president for finance on a regular basis.

Martin's empathy and organizational awareness set him apart from most of the other division heads, and he became one of the most respected managers in the firm. Whereas other managers often encountered obstacles from finance and accounting when they tried to move ahead with a project, Martin always found the "bean counters" to be cooperative and supportive. The CEO, grateful that Martin kept him so well informed about important matters, increasingly came to trust and rely on Martin.

Organizational awareness, like many of the other competencies, can get people in trouble if it is not tempered by other qualities. People who score high in organizational awareness but low in empathy and self-awareness are political animals who tend to alienate many of those with whom they work. They may succeed in the short run, but over time they generate so much mistrust, conflict, and resentment that they are likely to trip up. Emotional intelligence involves a blend of competencies, and organizational awareness is just one of them.

DIMENSION 4: SOCIAL SKILLS

Influence is another competency that distinguishes superior performers from others. People with this competency are skilled at winning over others. They know how to fine-tune presentations to appeal to the listener, and they are able to build support for policies and projects by developing coalitions. They have a knack for sensing what kinds of appeals will persuade pivotal decision makers.

Not surprisingly, influence is particularly important for all levels of management. It is one of the competencies that most strongly distinguish superior managers from others (Boyatzis 1982). Influence can be important in almost any job. Scientists and engineers who are brilliant technically may be relatively ineffective if they are not able to communicate their ideas in ways that convince others.

Influence is an emotional competency because it involves the ability to manage one's own emotions and those of others. Research on nonverbal behavior has shown that people who use facial expressions, voice modulation, gestures, and body movements to transmit emotion are better able to influence others (Friedman et al. 1980). Also, influence often involves establishing rapport, and EI is crucial for building the kind of rapport necessary for influence.

Influence is another competency that works best when combined with others. In the absence of empathy and self-control, skill in influence can become self-centered manipulation. Those who use influence to advance their own interests to the detriment of others sometimes can be successful, but they usually get into trouble sooner or later. Moreover, they can be extremely costly for the organization.

Closely related to influence is *leadership*. People with this competency are able to articulate and arouse enthusiasm for a shared vision and mission. They step forward to lead when needed, regardless of their position. They also are able to guide the performance of others while holding them accountable. They do all this primarily in the way they use emotion. Effective leaders strongly influence an organization's emotional tone. They express emotion in ways that inspire others.

Particularly effective leaders often are described as charismatic. Charisma depends on three factors: feeling strong emotions, expressing those emotions forcefully, and being an emotional sender rather than a receiver (Wasielewski 1985). Thus, the essence of good leadership is knowing how to manage and express emotion in ways that inspire peak performance in others.

Effective leaders recognize that emotions are contagious, and positive emotion leads to superior performance. In one study, a group of volunteers played the role of managers who had come together in a group to allocate bonuses to their subordinates. A trained actor was planted among them, and he always spoke first. In some groups he projected cheerful enthusiasm or relaxed warmth. In other groups he was depressed and sluggish or hostile and irritable. Not only was the actor able to infect the rest of the group with his emotion, but good feelings in the actor led to greater cooperation, fairness, and overall group performance. Even objective measures showed that the cheerful groups were better able to distribute the money fairly and in ways that helped the organization (Barsade 1998; Barsade and Gibson 1998).

A study of superior leaders in the U.S. Navy found that the greatest difference between them and average leaders was in their emotional style. The most effective leaders were more positive and outgoing, more emotionally expressive and dramatic, warmer, and more sociable. They also were friendlier and more democratic, and they were more appreciative and trustful than average leaders (Bachman 1988).

Effective leaders, however, also know when to be assertive, and they are not uncomfortable with confrontation or anger. They are able to take a stand, and they are clear and firm when necessary. They set high standards for performance and insist that people meet them. They do not rely heavily on toughness. They use more positive methods of influence first.

Leading the Way Into the Age of Personal Computers

Many of the features of modern computers that we take for granted came out of a single group: the Computer Science Laboratory at Xerox's Palo Alto Research Center (PARC). During the 1970s, that creative group developed the technology that eventually became the basis of both the MacIntosh and Windows operating systems. In addition, they created the first easy-to-learn word-processing program, the first local area network, and the first laser printer.

Although these creative accomplishments owe much to the individual contributions of several scientists, considerable credit goes to the individual who put together the group and led them: Bob Taylor. As one observer put it, "Without Taylor, it would have been chaos. He created the ideal environment for basic computer research, a setting so near to perfect that it enabled four dozen people to invent much of the computer technology we have today" (Cringely 1992).

Taylor's genius lay in part in his ability to facilitate others rather than manage or supervise them. He was not himself a computer scientist. As one of the scientists who worked at PARC said, he knew how to "get really great people together and manage the social dynamic. Managing the environment was what he was good at" (Bennis and Biederman 1997). For example, Taylor imposed very few rules on this creative group of scientists, but the one rule that could not be violated involved the weekly meeting. At this time, everyone in the lab came together to exchange valuable information about what they were learning and doing. It was also the place where members of the team dealt with their disagreements and conflicts.

Taylor's leadership ability also involved taking on the larger system when necessary. He was a strong advocate for his group—so strong, in fact, that he was willing to "sacrifice his career to protect his group" (Bennis and Biederman 1997). Taylor's willingness to champion the group's cause engendered fierce loyalty on the part of the members of the team.

Perhaps most important was Taylor's highly emotional commitment to the group and its work. "Taylor brought an almost religious zeal to his work of advancing the state of computing. Tirelessness, certainty of the importance of the task, unwavering focus—these were the qualities that Taylor brought to PARC and that he either recognized or inspired (probably some of both) in others" (Bennis and Biederman 1997).

Another social competency linked to superior performance in organizations is *change catalyst*. People with this competency are effective in mobilizing others toward change. They are skilled in developing coalitions of support and in anticipating and reducing sources of resistance. This competency actually represents an amalgam of several competencies, because an effective change catalyst is someone with high levels of self-confidence, initiative and innovation, influence, and leadership. The effective change catalyst also must possess a great deal of organizational awareness, and, of course, adaptability is also important.

The change catalyst has one other quality not yet mentioned: a real passion for that particular change whatever it might be. Few change efforts have much chance of success unless there is at least one person in the organization who is passionate about the change effort. As the pace of change has quickened during the last decade in American organizations, as the advantage increasingly has gone to those that change rather than those that remain stable, this competency has become important for both individual and organizational success.

Another competency that is important for effective performance is *communication.* People with this competency listen well and welcome the sharing of information. They foster open communication, and they are receptive to both bad news and good.

Skill in communication requires more than just the ability to understand the words used by others and to convey one's own words clearly. Communication is an emotional competency, because it depends in part on the ability to convey mood and meaning. Effective communicators are able to express a range of feelings in constructive ways. Superior leaders, for example, communicate clearly if they are pleased with what a subordinate has done, and they also communicate clearly when they are not pleased.

Effective communication also requires empathy. The key to good communication is good listening, which involves listening to more than just the words. Good listeners are able to "listen with a third ear," to hear what the other person is feeling and saying.

Communication also builds on the competency of self-control. For instance, a study of middle- and upper-level managers found that those who scored best as communicators were able to adopt a calm, composed manner no matter what their emotional state (Walter V. Clarke Associates 1996). Those who are preoccupied with their own feelings find it difficult to tune into the feelings of others, and this preoccupation makes for poor communication.

Communication always has been important for sales and managerial roles, but it is becoming increasingly important for most other positions, as well. For example, those in technical roles who stand out as superior performers are particularly effective communicators. Star computer consultants not only possess the technical expertise necessary for their work, they also are effective in hearing what their users and clients need, and they are skilled in communicating back to them technical information in ways that make it accessible and easy to understand. The technician who can make it sound simple is often worth his or her weight in gold.

Another valuable social competency is *conflict management.* People with this competency are able to spot potential conflict, bring it into the open, and help defuse it. They encourage debate and open discussion; they do not shy away from disagreement. They also have a knack for handling difficult people and tense situations with tact and diplomacy. They are adept at orchestrating win-win solutions when there is a conflict.

Like other social competencies, conflict management builds on many of the other competencies already considered. First, people with this competency tend to be especially aware of their own emotions, because it is those emotional reactions that help them to sense potentially disruptive conflicts long before others do. Conflict management also requires self-confidence and self-control; without these competencies, people are likely to avoid dealing with conflicts and miss opportunities to resolve them. Skill in negotiating also calls for flexibility, and people who are more adaptable tend to be better at managing conflict. Empathy and organizational awareness can be invaluable in helping people sense what the underlying issues in a conflict are likely to be, a key to finding a mutually satisfactory solution. Finally, skill in conflict management hinges upon the abilities to communicate effectively and to influence others.

Resolving Conflict Creatively

Matt had been a school psychologist for several years. He enjoyed counseling students and their families, but he did not like testing, report writing, or attending meetings. In this respect, he was like many other school psychologists. The difference was that Matt figured out a way to eliminate those aspects of the job that he did not find rewarding, and he did it in a way that greatly benefited his school district.

The opportunity came, strangely enough, when the school board faced a budget shortfall. To balance the budget, they had to cut the counselor positions in the elementary schools. Many principals, teachers, and parents were unhappy, but the school board saw no alternative. Matt, however, did.

He proposed to his boss that they develop a counselor internship program in the district. Graduate students from counseling programs at local colleges could work in the elementary schools to fulfill practicum requirements, and Matt would supervise them. The only cost would be hiring a part-time psychologist to do the testing and report writing that Matt would not be able to do while he was running the internship program. His boss encouraged him to write up a proposal and submit it to the school board. The beleaguered board members welcomed this inexpensive way of restoring counseling services in the elementary schools, and they quickly voted to approve the proposal.

At the end of the first year, Matt took the initiative to conduct an evaluation of the new program and wrote a report for the school board in which he presented data showing its popularity and usefulness. The board was pleased with this feedback, and they voted to allocate a small stipend for the counselor interns the following year, which made it easier for Matt to recruit high-quality people for the program.

Matt still was doing more testing and paperwork than he preferred, and so he looked for ways to expand the program. This was not difficult to do, because not every school had a counselor intern. Matt went to the principals who had counselor interns in their schools during the prior two years and told them that he would have to put interns in different schools during the next year unless the principals came up with money to cover expansion of the program. Matt also pointed out to them that they could use some of their federal grant money for this purpose. The principals readily agreed, and Matt was able to expand the program while further enriching his job.

Two trends in the contemporary workplace make conflict management an increasingly important competency. The first is the pressure and turbulence that accompany the massive changes that have occurred. As competitive pressures and technological change engulf organizations, as consolidation and downsizing continue unabated into a third decade, people become more impatient and less tolerant of themselves and others. Conflict in such a context is inevitable.

The other trend is diversity. The advantages of a diverse work-force are clear, but along with diversity comes conflict. The star performers are those who can get the most out of diversity, and that requires a willingness to face, rather than avoid, conflict and to resolve conflict in mutually satisfying ways whenever possible. Those who have this competency are valuable to any organization.

Stars also tend to excel at another social competency: *collaboration and building bonds*. People with this competency cultivate and maintain extensive informal networks composed of individuals who can provide them with a variety of information and expertise when they need it. They also are adept at balancing a focus on the task with attention to relationships. They are willing to share plans, information, and resources with others, and they promote a friendly, cooperative climate wherever they go.

The ability to network and collaborate with others has never been more important. For many years, Robert Kelley of Carnegie Mellon University has been asking people in a variety of organizations and jobs about what percentage of the knowledge needed to do their job is stored in their own heads. In 1986, the answer typically was 75 percent. By 1997, it was only 15 to 20 percent (Kelley 1998). As John Seely Brown (Goleman 1998), the chief scientist at Xerox Corporation, says, "Ideas don't come from a lone head, but from collaboration." People who recognize this fact and reach out to collaborate with others make significant contributions to their organizations. They also are more likely to succeed personally.

There are many ways, of course, to get information that is in other people's heads when working on a problem or a difficult task. Using an informal network tends to be the most efficient way. Superior performers are the ones who devote considerable time to developing a large and rich network of contacts to which they can turn. As a result, the stars get the answers sooner. In fact, for every hour a star spends in seeking information through a network, an average person spends three to five hours gathering the same information (Kelley 1998).

Consider the case of two engineers who are working on a technical problem and hit a snag. The first one spends several hours trying to come up with the answer on his own, poring over technical manuals, surfing the Web, and just plain obsessing about it. Eventually he calls someone he does not know well to ask for help, but that person is not in and does not return his call for a couple of days. The second engineer uses a different strategy. She thinks about the many work-related friendships she has developed and identifies two or three individuals who probably have the information she needs. She picks up the phone and leaves messages, and because she has developed a bond with these people, they return her call within an hour. In this example, the engineer who has developed an extensive social network solves the problem much more quickly than the one who relies more heavily on his own resources.

Collaboration is especially important in management. In a study by Manchester Incorporated, 82 percent of HR executives said that the failure "to build partnerships with peers and subordinates was the most common reason for the premature departure of a newly appointed manager" (Sweeney 1999).

Putting It All Together

Virtuoso performance in the workplace usually involves the combination of several different emotional competencies, as the following example suggests. The competencies that were used are indicated in parentheses.

Shortly after joining Tandem Computers as a junior staff analyst, Michael Iem became aware of the market trend away from mainframe computers to networks that linked workstations and personal computers (service orientation). Iem realized that unless Tandem

responded to the trend, its products would become obsolete (initiative and innovation). He still had to convince Tandem's managers that
their old emphasis on mainframes was no longer appropriate (influence) and then develop a system using new technology (leadership,
change catalyst). He spent four years showing off his new system to
customers and company sales personnel before the new network
applications were fully accepted (self-confidence, self-control,
achievement drive). Iem's emotional intelligence was a major factor
in Tandem's ability to adapt to the turbulent changes in the computer
industry (Richman 1994).

The last competency is *team capabilities*. People with this
competency draw all members of a group into active participation. They also are skilled in building team identity and commitment. They have the ability to keep the group working well
together. They protect the group and its reputation. Team capability is another competency that has become especially important in recent years. In fact, the group now is the fundamental
unit of the organization in many ways. Organizational effectiveness and productivity often are affected more by how well groups
function than by how well individuals function. What this means
is that the productivity gains associated with high-performing
teams can be much greater than those associated with high-
performing individuals.

For example, at one polyester-fiber plant, each of the top 10
teams produced 30 percent more fiber in a year than other teams
doing the same work. That difference meant an economic value
added of $9.8 million (Spencer 1997). These were manufacturing
teams; high-performing teams at top organizational tiers offer
even greater payoffs.

In effective teams, turnover and absenteeism are low and productivity is high (Moreland, Argote, and Krishnan 1998). What
makes a team work well? Research on team effectiveness suggests
that it depends on more than just the cognitive ability and technical skills of the individual members. In fact, in one study,
teams made up of individuals with high IQs performed worse

than teams whose average IQ was lower (Belbin 1982, 1996). The vital difference between superior teams and others depends on the members' relationships (Williams and Sternberg 1988). Those who are able to develop positive working relationships and esprit de corps within a team provide enormous value to both the team and the organization. Therefore, it is not surprising that the inability to lead a team was a frequent cause of failure among top American and European executives (Leslie and van Velsor 1996).

The ability to make teams work well represents, in many ways, a culmination of EI, for it is based upon and draws from almost all of the other social and emotional competencies. People who are gifted at bringing a team to new levels of achievement excel in self-awareness and self-management. They also stand out in social awareness and a variety of social skills. High-performing teams make it particularly clear why the competencies associated with EI are so vital for healthy, productive, and competitive organizations.

Exceptional Leadership Competencies— A Case Study From History

In 1914, Sir Ernest Shackleton set out on the last great challenge in polar exploration. The North and South Poles had already been conquered. Shackleton's goal was to cross the continent of Antarctica— the only continent that had not yet been traversed. Lansing (1959), quoted herein, chronicled the expedition from the expedition members' journals.

Leading 27 men across this frozen wasteland would have been a major accomplishment even if things had gone according to plan, but they did not. Shortly after crossing the Antarctic Circle, the *Endurance,* their ship, became trapped in the ice. They had to wait for the ice to recede so that they could continue their journey. Unfortunately, before that happened, the moving plates of ice destroyed the *Endurance,* and they had to abandon her. At that point, Shackleton set a new goal: travel hundreds of miles across ice and storm-tossed seas back to civilization (adaptability). Not only did he ultimately succeed, but also he did so without losing a single member of the expedition.

Certainly luck played a role, but much of the credit goes to Shackleton's leadership. "There can be little doubt that Shackleton, in his way, was an extraordinary leader of men...He had a talent—a genius even—that he shared with only a handful of men throughout history—genuine leadership...He was, as one of his men put it, 'the greatest leader that ever came on God's earth, bar none.'"

An analysis of that leadership reveals that their survival largely had to do with emotional intelligence. It began with Shackleton's recognition that this was the kind of situation in which his leadership abilities would flourish (self-knowledge). It was only in extreme situations that his leadership qualities emerged (initiative and innovation).

Shackleton's initial plan for the expedition was "purposeful, bold, and neat. He had not the slightest doubt that the expedition would achieve its goal" (self-confidence). Lansing also describes Shackleton as having a "monstrous ego and implacable drive" (achievement drive).

The ability to select the right person for the right job requires great emotional intelligence (organizational awareness, leadership). Shackleton's method for selecting the members of the expedition relied heavily on emotional dynamics rather than a careful and lengthy process of gathering data. "Shackleton's intuition for selecting compatible men rarely failed."

To save himself and all of his men, Shackleton often had to keep his emotions in check (self-control): "He was tormented by thoughts, both of what happened and what might have happened...He was careful, however, not to betray his disappointment to the men..."

Shackleton also seemed to have an uncanny ability to read others on an emotional level (empathy), and he used this skill to ensure that morale and cohesiveness within the group remained high (team capabilities, collaboration and building bonds). He was "intensely watchful for potential troublemakers who might nibble away at the unity of the group" (organizational awareness).

Another example of how Shackleton understood others' emotional needs was the way in which he treated Hurley, one of the members of the expedition. He sensed that the man "needed to be made to feel important," and that if he felt slighted, he might spread discontent among the others (team capabilities, conflict management). So Shackleton "frequently sought his opinion, and he was careful to compliment him on his work. He also assigned Hurley to his own tent, which appealed to Hurley's snobbishness and also minimized his opportunities for gathering other latent malcontents around himself."

Shackleton was also highly effective in the way he shaped others' emotions, beginning with the two-year effort to secure funding for the expedition. Shackleton was successful because of his "great personal charm." In his appeals, he would often play on England's national pride, pointing out that the Americans already had reached the North Pole, and the Norwegians had narrowly beaten the British in the race to the South Pole (influence, communication).

Shackleton was particularly effective at using dramatic gestures to communicate strong messages to the men (influence, communication). When their ship was destroyed and they had to set out on a long journey by foot back to civilization, Shackleton announced that they would have to travel light if they were to survive."...He reached under his parka and took out a gold cigarette case and several gold sovereigns and threw them into the snow at his feet. Then he took his Bible, ripped out three pages to keep with him, and "laid the Bible in the snow and walked away."

Even though the expedition was highly diverse in social class, nearly everyone liked one another and got along: "It was remarkable that there were not more cases of friction among the men, especially after the Antarctic night set in...But instead of getting on each other's nerves, the entire party seemed to become more close-knit." Shackleton was largely responsible for this (leadership, collaboration and building bonds, empathy).

The *Endurance* had set sail from England in August 1914, and she became trapped in the Antarctic ice in January 1915. The men's ordeal continued until rescue finally came in August of 1916. Many factors enabled them to survive, but by far the most important was the leadership of Ernest Shackleton. His emotional intelligence ultimately saved the lives of 28 men.

Competencies can be developed throughout life. The next chapter describes each of the model programs to help the reader envision the guidelines in practice. The remainder of this book shows how people at any age can improve their emotional competency and, in so doing, achieve a more satisfying and productive life—at work and at home.

3

EI

The Model Programs

The Consortium for Research on Emotional Intelligence in Organizations identified more than a dozen model programs that are based on very different approaches to promoting or developing EI in the workplace. What makes these programs different from other training and development programs?

To be considered a model, a program had to be intended for adult workers, and it had to target one or more of the emotional and social competencies associated with EI. Strong evaluation data had to document its effectiveness. The consortium applied the following criteria to decide whether a program could qualify as a model:

- *Replication:* The program has been delivered more than once.
- *Sample size:* The program has been provided to, and evaluated for, more than just a few individuals.
- *Control group:* The evaluation research included a control group.
- *Outcome measures:* Data is available on competency development, performance, or financial outcomes.
- *Multiple data points:* Pre- and posttraining measures were available.

ACHIEVEMENT MOTIVATION TRAINING

This model primarily targets the achievement drive competency. Originally developed by Harvard psychologist David McClelland and his colleagues at Hay/McBer (Miron and McClelland 1979), it has been used in many different settings for many different types of individuals, including corporate executives, small business entrepreneurs, minority business professionals, business school students, police officers, and social workers. It also has been used in other countries. In fact, it was first used in 1963 with business professionals in India.

McClelland's achievement motivation training program has been offered on numerous occasions, and several evaluation studies have documented its effectiveness. Training methods used during this five-day training program include lecture, discussion, simulation, case exercises, and development of an action plan to be used in the home organization.

The results of one evaluation showed that program participants evidenced a significantly higher rate of advancement within their companies when compared to a control group. In another evaluation study, an achievement motivation training program targeted at small business owners was shown to be effective in influencing business performance. Results of a cost-benefit analysis of this government-sponsored program showed that the net increase in tax revenues due to the increased profitability of the targeted businesses more than paid for the program.

CAREGIVER SUPPORT PROGRAM

The caregiver support program (CSP) was designed specifically for human service workers, particularly those working in group homes and halfway houses for mentally ill or developmentally disabled individuals (Heaney, Price, and Rafferty 1995). The primary goal of the program was to teach the participants skills that will help them cope more effectively with the stresses associated with their work. It helped participants develop several self-management and social skills competencies, including adaptability, communication, collaboration and building bonds, conflict management, and team capabilities.

The program was designed by staff at the Michigan Prevention Research Center, and it has been implemented numerous times throughout the state of Michigan. To date, more than 2,000 human service workers have participated in it. A unique aspect of the program was that staff and their managers are trained together. One staff member and the manager from each home attended the CSP sessions with the expectation that they would train the rest of the staff on the skills and concepts they had learned.

This program was structured according to social learning theory with emphasis on modeling and rehearsal of new behaviors. The content of the training included helping participants understand existing helping networks, strengthening those networks, exploring how social support from others might help solve problems and reduce stress at work, and mapping their own strengths and weaknesses in their own social networks at work. Participants learned to refine their interpersonal skills associated with exchanging social support with others, clarifying misunderstandings, giving constructive feedback, and asking others for help.

Results of a program evaluation show participants reported higher levels of supervisory support, experienced higher levels of praise and feedback, and had more contact with co-workers.

EMOTIONAL COMPETENCE TRAINING PROGRAM

A small group of staff in the life insurance division at American Express Financial Advisors originally developed this program in the early 1990s. It grew out of an effort to discover why some clients who needed life insurance were not buying it. Research suggested that a major barrier was the financial advisors' emotional reactions to the process. Consequently, the company developed and tested a training program designed to help the advisors cope more effectively with the emotional conflicts that they sometimes encountered in working with clients around life insurance matters.

A major goal of the program was to help managers to become emotional coaches for their direct reports. The training was designed to help the managers more fully appreciate the role that emotion plays in the workplace and to develop a greater awareness of their own emotional reactions and those of their direct reports. They also learn how to communicate with their direct reports in ways that help them to manage their emotions more effectively.

The pilot program eventually became the emotional competence training (ECT) program. It targeted virtually every aspect of EI but particularly the core competencies of emotional self-awareness, self-control, empathy, communication, and conflict management. The leadership version of the program offered to managers also helps build the "developing others" competency.

The company recently completed an evaluation study suggesting that participation in the program contributed to increased sales revenue. The advisors of trained managers grew their businesses by 18.1 percent compared to 16.2 percent for those whose managers were untrained.

EMPATHY TRAINING FOR MEDICAL STUDENTS

Technological advances in medicine, along with changes in the way medical care is delivered, have been a mixed blessing. One of the apparent costs of such change has been increasing dissatisfaction with the way that medical personnel treat patients. Research in the early 1960s began to document the tendency for medical students to become increasingly callous and dehumanizing in their behavior towards patients during their training. Eventually, medical schools and teaching hospitals began to develop experimental programs designed to train future physicians to be more empathic and sensitive in their interactions with patients. The programs primarily target the competencies of empathy and communication.

An example of such a program is the one developed and evaluated in the pediatrics ward at a large university hospital in Israel (Kramer, Ber, and Moore 1989). The participants were fifth-year medical students (students in their first year of clinical training). In addition to the students, 10 doctor-tutors also were included in the program. The doctor-tutors participated in a supporting medical interview workshop. Following the workshop, the doctor-tutors helped deliver the training to some of the medical students.

Today many medical schools include such programs as part of their training (Caruso, Nieman, and Gracely 1994; Evans et al. 1991; Greco et al. 1998; Mason et al. 1988; Roter et al. 1998). One version consists of 10 90-minute sessions held twice weekly for five weeks. Each of the 10 sessions is structured around a specific topic such as the diagnosis of a severe disease, family counseling, and chronic disease. Results of an evaluation showed that the program improved empathy and communication skills in program participants when compared with a control group.

EXECUTIVE COACHING

Executive coaching has become a popular method for promoting EI in organizations (Peterson, Uranowitz, and Hicks 1996); however, only a few rigorous evaluations have been conducted for such programs. An exception is the program developed and offered through PDI. This program has served over 4,000 individuals, and it provides a good model of this type of development. Depending on the individual, coaching can target any of the EI competencies, but typically it focuses on the self-awareness, self-management, and social skills competencies.

The individual coaching for effectiveness (ICE) program is an individualized program targeted at executives and middle managers, and it is delivered by highly trained individuals (Peterson 1996). About 80 percent of their coaches have doctoral degrees in psychology. The others have master's degrees in psychology or social work. In addition, new coaches go through their own development programs, which may include close, weekly supervision for some.

The typical participant goes through an initial one- or two-day diagnostic assessment and feedback session, followed by the coaching phase, which involves about one day of training per month for the next six months. The typical participant receives about 50 hours of intensive one-on-one work. Specific behavioral learning objectives are developed for each individual. These objectives are defined in terms of expected on-the-job behaviors. Each person's goals are unique, based on an integration of the organization's description of the person's needs and the results of the diagnostic assessment. Ratings of each behavior are collected from the participant, the coach, and the participant's supervisor before coaching. These ratings are compared with scores immediately after training and six months after training is complete.

Results of the evaluation indicated that all three ratings showed improvement on behaviors targeted for coaching. Moreover, these improvements were maintained over time as evidenced by a follow-up evaluation. To date over 2,500 executives and middle managers have gone through this program.

HUMAN RELATIONS TRAINING

The earliest example of training in emotional and social competence in organizations was called human relations training.

Between 1950 and 1975 hundreds of human relations training programs were offered to thousands of managers in American organizations. Most of these efforts were not evaluated, and many were disappointing in their lack of lasting effects. One program, however, stands out as an exception.

The managerial human relations training program described by Hand, Richards, and Slocum (1973) was developed at Pennsylvania State University. It was an off-the-shelf program conducted by the continuing education division. Through that division, it was delivered numerous times in firms throughout an area comprising several states. The objective of the program was to encourage participants to use principles of human relations in their dealings with employees. More specifically, the program designers sought to increase participants' use of consideration and initiating structure. Thus, the program targeted the emotional competencies of self-awareness, empathy, and leadership.

The training consisted of 28 90-minute sessions conducted weekly. Divided into phases, phase I of the training focused on discussions of leaders, leadership, followership, and leadership styles. Phase II, the largest component of the training, was devoted to experiential learning exercises such as self-ratings on the managerial grid, partition exercises, judgment, in-basket, listening, and interview exercises. Phase III of the training focused on motivation theories.

Pre- and posttraining measures of self-awareness, sensitivity to the needs of others, and leadership styles were completed. Behavior ratings by supervisors and subordinates were also collected. Evaluation was done 90 days and 18 months after completion of the program. The training was found to be effective in changing attitudes and behaviors and these changes were related to increased managerial effectiveness. Managers who completed the training increased their self-awareness, were more sensitive to the needs of others, and focused on developing mutual trust with their employees. Subordinates reported that they had better rapport and communication with managers who had completed the training.

JOBS PROGRAM

The main objective of this program was to enhance productive job-seeking skills and self-confidence for the unemployed. Short-term goals included fortifying job seekers' ability to resist demoralization and to persist in the face of barriers and setbacks. The long-term goal was to help people seek employment in settings that maximize economic, social, and psychological rewards. The program helped participants maintain high levels of motivation, become more adept at finding job leads and interviewing for jobs, and cope with the setbacks and frustrations associated with job seeking (Caplan, Vinokur, and Price 1996; Price and Vinokur 1995; Vinokur and Schul 1997). The program contributed to the development of several social and emotional competencies: self-awareness, accurate self-assessment, self-confidence, adaptability, self-control, conscientiousness, empathy, organizational awareness, influence, communication, and collaboration and building bonds.

A group of psychologists associated with the Michigan Prevention Research Center at the University of Michigan developed the JOBS program. The Prevention Research Center was involved because another goal of the program was to prevent depression and other psychological problems associated with unemployment. Initially the program was implemented in Michigan with participants recruited from the Michigan Employment Security Commission. Since then the program has been adopted in several other states and foreign countries.

Results of an evaluation indicated that program participants found employment sooner than a control group. A follow-up study showed continued beneficial effects on monthly earnings, level of employment, and episodes of employer and job changes.

LEADERLAB

Beginning in 1991, the Center for Creative Leadership (CCL) launched an open-enrollment program called LeaderLab, which endeavors to help upper- and middle-level managers and executives become more effective leaders (LeaderLab 1994; Young and Dixon 1996). Each participant is assigned to a process advisor (PA) who serves as a personal coach throughout the program's evolution. The program focuses on enhancing emotional competencies such as self-awareness, leadership, accurate self-assessment, initiative and innovation, achievement drive, change catalyst, and team capabilities.

The program is implemented over a six-month period and meets at the Center for Creative Leadership twice, the initial session being six days with a subsequent four-day session held three months later. Participants are encouraged to implement an action plan developed during the initial six-day training session over the interim period at their home organizations. Training during the second training period focuses on ways to modify and improve the initial action plan.

Results of an evaluation based on data collected from participants and their co-workers shows participant improvement in self-awareness, social awareness, self-regulation, and social skills following participation in the program.

SELF-MANAGEMENT TRAINING

Training in self-management initially was developed and used by clinical psychologists. The underlying premise was that individuals who need to change are more likely to succeed if they are in control of the change process. Rather than have a psychologist use behavioral principles to bring about change, the individual should be taught those principles and helped to apply them on his or her own. When people take charge of their own change program, they are more likely to feel efficacious, and change should be more lasting than if they feel that someone else is in charge. Self-management programs thus can affect several emotional competencies, including accurate self-assessment, self-confidence, self-control, conscientiousness, reliability, and achievement drive.

One of the first workplace applications of self-management training occurred in a unionized state government agency (Frayne and Latham 1987; Latham and Frayne 1989). The participants were employees who had records of frequent absences. The employees (carpenters, electricians, and painters) received eight weekly, one-hour group sessions during which they were taught how to:

- set proximal and distal goals for job attendance
- write a behavioral contract with themselves for administering self-chosen reinforcers and punishers
- self-monitor their attendance behavior
- administer their selected incentives
- brainstorm potential problems in implementing their plans and come up with potential solutions.

An evaluation of the program revealed that the program increased participant self-efficacy and job attendance.

STRESS MANAGEMENT TRAINING

Stress management programs have become popular in the workplace over the last two decades. Not all are effective, but evaluation research suggests that the ones that have been well-designed and carefully implemented not only reduce employee stress and improve health but also result in bottom-line benefits.

One example is Corning's holistic stress management program. The program evolved out of a collaborative partnership between Corning and the National Institute for Occupational Safety and Health (NIOSH). Like most such programs, it affected social and emotional competencies, such as self-confidence, self-control, communication, and adaptability. The program took place in approximately 50 locations and involved about 3,000 individuals. The initial goal of the program was to address the sources of nonproductive stress on the job (Monroy et al. 1997).

Workers were provided introductory information on stress through multiple channels ranging from in-house media communications to formal symposia featuring well-known researchers in the field. A series of weekly training sessions taught workers stress management skills: muscle relaxation, biofeedback, meditation, and cognitive restructuring. Results of a program evaluation showed significant changes on measures of stress symptoms and stress management skills after eight weeks of training.

SUPERVISORY TRAINING BASED ON BEHAVIOR MODELING

Ever since the seminal work of Goldstein and Sorcher (1974), behavior modeling has been used to train supervisory personnel in a number of different settings. The method is based on Bandura's (1977) social learning theory, which suggests that people learn in part by observing and then emulating models. One example of this approach was the interaction modeling program (IMP), developed more than 20 years ago by Developmental Dimensions International (DDI). Targeted for managers and supervisors in various occupations (including health care, communications, education, and manufacturing), IMP strove to improve supervisory skills in areas such as productivity, handling employee conflict and complaints, employee absenteeism, and overcoming resistance to change. The method did so through videotaped models of positive behavior, participant practice, and on-the-job application. The program addresses accurate self-assessment, adaptability, initiative, innovation, empathy, communication, and other social and emotional competencies (Pesuric and Byham 1996).

To date, more than three million managers have been trained through the interaction management and skill practices program. There now are many different versions of this learning approach that have been evaluated and found to be effective in promoting social and emotional competence.

In one study, a major manufacturing firm assessed the effects of a modeling-based training program by evaluating employees' lost-time accidents before and after their supervisors were trained. Lost-time accidents were reduced by 50 percent. Investigation of formal grievances and productivity were also evaluated. Formal grievances were reduced from an average of 15 per year to three per year. The plant exceeded productivity goals by $250,000.

Other behavior modeling training programs have achieved similar, impressive results. For example, an IMP was implemented with a group of supervisors in a forest products company (Porras and Anderson 1981). The results indicated that within two months following completion of the IMP, the trained supervisors had significantly increased their use of all five target behaviors.

Finally, another evaluation of a behavior modeling program in the transportation industry showed decreased turnover, absenteeism, and overtime.

TRAINING IN CONFLICT MANAGEMENT FOR POLICE OFFICERS

During the 1960s, social scientists began to recognize the extent to which police are involved in interpersonal conflicts. Research indicated that many police injuries occur when they intervene in conflicts between individuals who know one another. Also, as mental institutions began to discharge their patients in large numbers (a trend referred to as deinstitutionalization), police were called upon more than ever to deal with complex psychological problems. In addition, changes in many inner-city communities put heavy strains on police-community relations, and many people believed that lack of skill in managing interpersonal conflict on the part of the police either caused or exacerbated such strain.

All of these trends led to growing interest in teaching police how to resolve interpersonal conflict more effectively. Initially such efforts met with considerable opposition from tradition-bound police departments steeped in a military culture. Such programs gradually gained acceptance, and today it would be difficult to find a large urban police department that has not used such training.

One of the first efforts to help police officers become more effective in managing interpersonal conflict was a program developed at the City University of New York (Zacker and Bard 1973). In addition to helping participants become more competent in conflict management, this program included training in the competencies of influence, communication, empathy, and self-awareness.

Training procedures for this group included group discussions, real-life simulations of interpersonal conflicts, role plays, and lectures. These activities were all designed to improve the participants' ability to manage interpersonal conflicts by providing learning experiences that promoted active involvement by each participant.

A comparison of program participants with controls found that for each criterion, program participants received the highest rank, denoting greatest improvement (or least decrement) on all 10 performance measures. For instance, officers participating in the program showed significantly higher case-clearance rates.

Participants also showed decreased absenteeism as evidenced by a danger-tension index, which is calculated as total arrests divided by total sick days.

WEATHERHEAD SCHOOL OF MANAGEMENT PROGRAM

The competency-based curriculum for a master's degree of business administration (M.B.A.) program at Case Western Reserve University's Weatherhead School of Management makes the promotion of social and emotional competence an integral part of a student's education. The faculty-driven curriculum change evolved to address the criticisms that graduate management education has encountered over the years. The program adds value by explicitly targeting social and emotional competencies that are related to superior managerial performance: accurate self-assessment, achievement drive, conflict management, empathy, self-confidence, networking (collaborating and building bonds), flexibility (adaptability), developing others, self-control, initiative and innovation, and social objectivity (communication) (Boyatzis 1982).

At the outset of M.B.A training, all students are required to participate in the managerial assessment and development course. The goals of this course are "to learn a method for assessing one's knowledge and abilities relevant to management," to develop "plans for acquiring new management-related knowledge and abilities throughout one's career," and to become more aware of "one's own values and the values of others" (Boyatzis 1994). The students go through in-depth assessment activities for two weeks followed by feedback and interpretation of assessment activities for the next seven weeks. The assessment results guide students in selecting appropriate coursework and internship experiences.

Several cohorts of students who have gone through the program now have been evaluated longitudinally. Students who have participated in the competency-based program have been compared to those who went through the traditional program. These comparisons suggest that the program helps promote positive change in many different social and emotional competencies, including initiative, flexibility, achievement drive, empathy, self-confidence, persuasiveness, networking, self-control, and group management.

DISCERNING BEST PRACTICES

Rigorous evaluations, further discussed in chapter 9, proved that each model program made business sense. Each one made significant, beneficial differences on the organizations' spreadsheets and on the organizations' performance.

The best-practice guidelines set down in this book were drawn from the model programs described here. This chapter contained thumbnail sketches of the model programs to help the reader interpret the guidelines in the context of the programs from which they evolved. This list is not exhaustive; the consortium is continuing to identify such programs and add them to a best-practice database. In addition, more complete information on the model programs is available on the consortium's Website at www.eiconsortium.org.

4

EI

The Path to Social and Emotional Learning

Much of the money currently being spent on training in the soft skills may be going to waste, but it need not be. Research on social and emotional learning, the psychology of behavioral change, and more than a dozen model programs with well-documented results prove that it is possible to help adults in the workplace become more emotionally competent. Too many efforts, however, are doomed to failure because they do not incorporate the elements necessary for effective social and emotional learning.

Consider the example of a large financial services company that wanted to train its new financial advisors to be more emotionally intelligent. Management believed that EI would help the advisors to be better attuned to the needs of their clients, and this would lead to more satisfied clients and, therefore, more business. The company developed a five-day training program spread out over three months. Evaluation data suggested that the program was effective; it helped the advisors sell more financial products. Those in charge of the training program for new advisors then decided to reduce the program to one day (about six hours).

As we will see, such a truncated program has little chance of success. For example, one of the competencies that the new advisors needed to develop was empathy—the ability to tune into their clients' feelings, to identify what those feelings are, and to use that information to help the clients develop more appropriate financial plans. If new advisors lacked empathy, they first needed to become aware of that deficiency. They also had to be convinced that this lack of empathy hindered their effectiveness as advisors. To make this leap in EI, the new advisors needed to be strongly motivated to improve their empathy. Furthermore, the advisors who lacked empathy had become accustomed to operating in the way they did. For many years, they had spent virtually every day of their lives thinking and acting in ways that lacked empathy. In other words, their lack of empathy was based on strong habits that were highly resistant to change. To become more empathetic in the way that they interacted with clients, these advisors needed to learn new ways of thinking and feeling, and then they needed several weeks, if not months, to practice diligently these new behaviors in a variety of situations, including meetings with clients.

Replacing one behavior with another is hard work, and the advisors' progress was not smooth and linear. Setbacks and reverses were encountered. During this learning period, the advisors needed ongoing support. A single, eight-hour training session in EI would do little to help the new advisors develop even a single competency that they needed to be superior performers.

The company spent millions of dollars on the program, and it will continue to do so until frustration and dissatisfaction with the lack of results become strong enough to bring about change. The truncated, one-day training program in EI reflects a lack of understanding about the difference between technical (cognitive) learning and emotional learning. For example, the new financial advisors had to learn a considerable amount of technical information during the training. They were able to learn much of it in eight hours of lecture, discussion, and practice exercises. They could learn quickly how to use financial data to design a personalized financial plan for a client. Such learning builds on cognitive abilities that they already possessed. It was clear to the advisors why such a skill is needed for the job, so motivation was not an issue. Emotional learning is different, though.

BIOLOGICAL BASIS FOR EI

At the level of the brain, there are some important differences between cognitive and emotional learning that training programs need to accommodate. Emotional incompetence often stems from habits learned early in life. These automatic habits are set in place as a normal part of living, as experience shapes the brain. People acquire a habitual repertoire of thought, feeling, and action, and the neural connections that support this repertoire become stronger. Connections that are not used become weaker (Edelman 1987). When habits are strong, the underlying neural connections become the brain's default option—what a person does automatically and spontaneously often with little or no awareness that a menu of possible responses is available. The behavior of the financial advisors who lacked empathy was a habitual pattern of neural responses to be overcome and replaced with a new pattern of thoughts, feelings, and actions.

Emotional capacities, empathy, for example, also differ from cognitive abilities in that they emanate from different parts of the brain. Cognitive abilities are based in the neocortex, which is evolutionarily the most recent part of the cerebral cortex. Social and emotional competencies involve the emotional centers of the brain, especially the amygdala. These parts of the brain are much older in evolutionary terms than is the neocortex (figure 4-1). Learning in the brain's emotional centers occurs not through words and ideas but through simple, repeated actions and vivid experiences.

Cognitive learning involves fitting new bits of information into existing frameworks of understanding. Emotional learning requires modification of the circuitry in the emotional parts of the brain. Changing habits is more challenging than simply adding new information to old.

Motivational factors also make social and emotional learning more difficult and complex than purely cognitive learning.

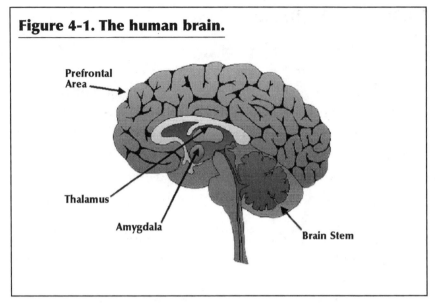

Figure 4-1. The human brain.

Prefrontal Area

Thalamus

Amygdala

Brain Stem

SOURCE: Reprinted with permission of Hay/McBer Associates, 2000.

Emotional learning often involves ways of thinking and acting that are more central to a person's identity. People who are told, for example, that they should learn a new word-processing program usually become less upset and defensive than if they are told that they should learn how to better control their tempers or become better listeners. The prospect of needing to develop greater emotional competence is a bitter pill for many to swallow and, therefore, is much more likely to generate resistance to change.

In many respects emotional and social learning is more like learning a physical skill. Both involve the older, preverbal areas of the brain. Deutsch (1994) showed how social and emotional learning is even more difficult than learning a physical skill such as playing tennis. Tennis novices receive continuous and clear feedback about whether they are performing adequately: If the ball is hit correctly, it will go in the proper direction at the right velocity. In contrast, no one is a novice when he or she starts training in conflict resolution or other social and emotional competencies; one always brings a host of preconceptions and modes of behavior that can get in the way of learning. Finally, in learning social and emotional skills, one must become attuned to how the social and cultural context influences the transfer of learning from one situation to another. Police officers, for example, may need to alter the way they apply conflict resolution skills from one neighborhood to another. For tennis players, differences in the social and cultural context have little effect on how one plays the game.

Because emotional learning differs from both cognitive and physical learning in several ways, it usually involves a long and sometimes difficult process requiring much practice and support. One-day seminars will not work. In fact, the superficiality and inadequacy of such programs tend to turn people in the organization against such training, making it more difficult to garner support for it in the future. What, then, is required to make EI training a success in terms of personal and business goals? How can deep-seated, long-held behaviors rooted in the brain's emotional centers be changed?

MODEL FOR EI-BASED LEARNING

Training and development efforts designed to increase emotional and social competence must incorporate a number of elements. Figure 4-2 is a model that incorporates the necessary elements into a set of guidelines, arranged in the form of a flowchart. The model synthesizes research and theory on organizational behavior, training and development, psychotherapy, and behavioral change. It is organized in a way that can help practitioners design effective learning processes and so help individuals meet personal goals and move businesses toward success.

The model represents the optimal process for helping individuals increase their emotional competence in personal and

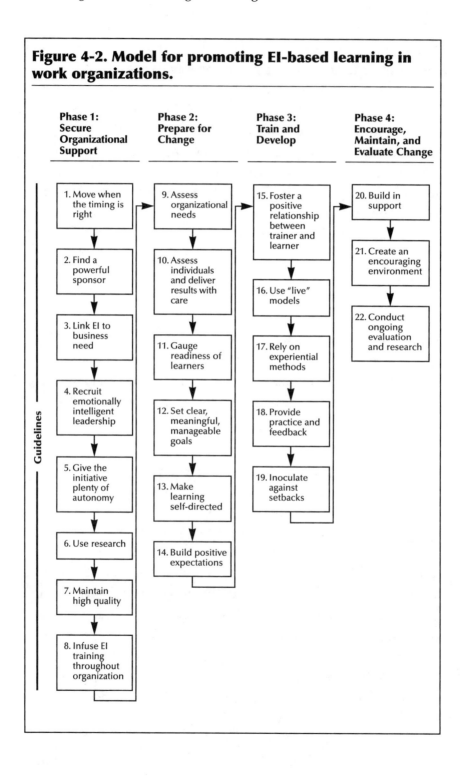

Figure 4-2. Model for promoting EI-based learning in work organizations.

Phase 1: Secure Organizational Support	Phase 2: Prepare for Change	Phase 3: Train and Develop	Phase 4: Encourage, Maintain, and Evaluate Change
1. Move when the timing is right	9. Assess organizational needs	15. Foster a positive relationship between trainer and learner	20. Build in support
2. Find a powerful sponsor	10. Assess individuals and deliver results with care	16. Use "live" models	21. Create an encouraging environment
3. Link EI to business need	11. Gauge readiness of learners	17. Rely on experiential methods	22. Conduct ongoing evaluation and research
4. Recruit emotionally intelligent leadership	12. Set clear, meaningful, manageable goals	18. Provide practice and feedback	
5. Give the initiative plenty of autonomy	13. Make learning self-directed	19. Inoculate against setbacks	
6. Use research	14. Build positive expectations		
7. Maintain high quality			
8. Infuse EI training throughout organization			

Guidelines

interpersonal contexts. The model suggests that the process for incorporating EI-based learning in the workplace consists of four basic phases.

The model begins with phase 1, which is a set of guidelines for introducing social and emotional learning into an organization and securing organizational buy-in. This phase encompasses the tasks necessary to develop support for what may be a new and unsettling idea: promoting emotional competence in the workplace.

Phase 2 involves preparation for change. Like phase 1, it occurs even before the individual begins formal learning. This phase, which is crucial for effective social and emotional learning, includes processes that are important for maximizing learners' motivation, according to previous research (Baldwin, Magjuka, and Loher 1991; Hicks and Klimoski 1987; Locke and Latham 1990; Prochaska, Norcross, and DiClemente 1994; Spencer and Spencer 1993). This preparation occurs at both the organizational and individual levels.

Phase 3, the actual training and development, covers the change process itself. It includes the processes that previous research on behavioral change suggests are important to help people change the way in which they view the world and deal with its social and emotional demands (Baldwin and Ford 1988; Bandura, Adams, and Beyer 1977; Ford 1978; Horvath and Symonds 1991; Kolb, Winter, and Berlew 1968; Komaki, Heinzmann, and Lawson 1980; Marx 1982; Spencer, McClelland, and Kelner 1997; Tannenbaum and Yukl 1992; Zacker and Bard 1973).

Phase 4 addresses what happens following the formal training experience. The activities of this phase are especially important for facilitating transfer, generalization, and maintenance of change. This phase determines whether the new behaviors will become a permanent part of the person's EI repertoire or be extinguished for lack of reinforcement. This phase also involves evaluation. Given the current state of knowledge about social and emotional learning and the complexity of programs designed to promote such learning, evaluation always should be part of the process. Making it an explicit part of the model recognizes this fact.

USING THE MODEL

The rest of this book works through the flowchart, discussing each of the guidelines in some detail. The guidelines also are presented in a concise format—a handy reference tool for practitioners—in appendix A. To amplify the guidelines, each chapter includes examples of how different model programs have incorporated the guidelines in practice. A list of assessment questions at the end of each chapter will help guide practitioners who are moving their organizations toward EI-based training.

It is not necessary to incorporate all of the guidelines or to follow the optimal process exactly to help people develop greater EI. Nevertheless, the more guidelines that a development effort incorporates, the more likely it is to be successful. The guidelines are synergistic in that each additional guideline that is incorporated multiplies the impact of a program. To put it another way, a program that incorporates six guidelines will be more than twice as effective as a program that incorporates only three guidelines.

5

Phase 1: Secure Organizational Support

Promoting EI in the workplace is often a new and unsettling idea for many people. For this reason, the way an organization launches EI training can affect the ultimate outcome in a significant way.

To learn more about the elements that contribute to successful implementation, we studied in depth the emotional competence training (ECT) developed by American Express Financial Advisors. We spent 50 hours interviewing more than 30 people who played important roles in developing the program. We also observed the delivery of the whole training program. As we learned more about the history of the program, we began to identify certain critical elements for gaining the organizational support necessary for successful implementation. We used these factors to articulate guidelines 1–8, which constitute phase 1 of the model for developing and

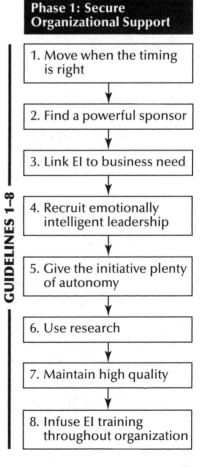

Phase 1: Secure Organizational Support

GUIDELINES 1–8

1. Move when the timing is right
2. Find a powerful sponsor
3. Link EI to business need
4. Recruit emotionally intelligent leadership
5. Give the initiative plenty of autonomy
6. Use research
7. Maintain high quality
8. Infuse EI training throughout organization

implementing EI training initiatives. In this chapter we present those guidelines with examples from the program.

GUIDELINE 1: MOVE WHEN THE TIMING IS RIGHT

At certain times in the life of any organization, the conditions will be more or less favorable for the implementation of EI training and development activities. Those who wish to establish such activities in their organization need to ask themselves whether the timing is right. Sometimes it may be necessary to wait until conditions are more favorable.

The ECT program benefited greatly from good timing. When a small group of people in the company first came together to develop the program, the company was doing very well. There was relatively little pressure or turbulence. This meant that the people involved, including the executive who initially sponsored it, could take some risks. If they had been concerned about every dollar they spent, something that then seemed as radical as EI training probably would not have been pursued.

Timing was also propitious in the way the program came to be linked to a high-profile reengineering project. This project began at about the same time as the EI training project did. Although they were two separate and seemingly unrelated projects, the developers of the EI project saw connections and emphasized them when they discussed their work with others. For example, the reengineering group focused on the factors that contributed to advisor success and turnover. It was not difficult to show a connection between the emotional competence of the advisors and their ability to remain in the job and be effective.

Timing was opportune in one other way. When the design team for the EI training completed the first pilot test and was ready to start offering the program throughout the company, a strong, corporation-wide training initiative for the salesforce had just begun. Much money suddenly was available for training of all sorts. This favorable climate for training did not last long; within a year, the amount of money began to diminish, and within three years the generous subsidies provided by the corporate office all but disappeared. Fortunately, by that time the program had become well established and known throughout the company.

GUIDELINE 2: FIND A POWERFUL SPONSOR

For better or worse, organizations tend to be political entities. The support of an influential executive is vital for a new, unconventional initiative such as EI training. Finding a powerful sponsor who can provide political protection and financial backing can make the difference between success and failure.

For the ECT, two powerful sponsors helped the program become established and gain widespread recognition. The first was Jim Mitchell, the senior vice president in charge of life insurance and annuities. He observed that the advisors did a good job of selling annuities and other financial products, but selling life insurance was not their strong suit. So, he brought together the four people who eventually developed the EI program and asked them to pinpoint the problem and create a solution. He gave them their own budget and six months with almost complete autonomy. They came up with an unexpected and unconventional answer: that both the clients' and the advisors' feelings about life insurance got in the way of life insurance sales. When they recommended that the solution was to provide the advisors with training in how to cope better with those feelings, there was much skepticism and eye-rolling. Mitchell often heard such comments as "Why do you want to allocate money for this touchy-feely garbage?" Nevertheless, he provided the protection that the project's designers needed to persevere and validate their findings.

Mitchell was a particularly effective sponsor because of his position and his solid track record. At the time, he was the head of the fastest-growing life insurance concern in the country, and he was viewed by many as a mover and a shaker in the insurance industry. Also, he was an actuary by training, and actuaries are viewed as anything but reckless or "flaky." All of these credentials gave him a great deal of credibility and clout. With this sponsorship, the new program was allowed to move ahead with its unconventional message.

After the pilot test and evaluation, Mitchell handed the program over to Doug Lennick, the senior vice president for sales, who became an even more enthusiastic sponsor. Lennick had been with the company for 20 years, starting as an advisor right out of college. From the beginning he was extraordinarily successful. Within a year he was asked to help train new advisors, and within two years he was promoted to district manager. His district was ranked best in the country for seven of eight years. He had been the executive in charge of sales for more than five years when he became the program's sponsor. He was viewed as an excellent sales leader, and he was very well regarded in the field and in the home office. Also, he headed up one of the most valued parts of the company. As one person put it, "New sales are what generates revenue for the company."

Lennick liked the program. He long had believed that emotions were crucial to selling. He was convinced that his own success had much to do with helping people deal with emotions. He even had written a book in which he discussed the importance of emotions and motivation in sales. Therefore, when he became the "owner" of the program, he gave it more than just a home and a budget. He became an advocate; he strongly plugged the program every time he spoke to a new group of advisors. Virtually everyone with whom we spoke said that this sponsor's support was crucial to the program's acceptance and survival. As one person said, "People in the field could have killed it—and they would have—without his support."

GUIDELINE 3: LINK EI TO BUSINESS NEED

Support for training and development in EI will increase if EI is clearly linked to a business need. People in the organization need to see it not as just a nice thing to do that makes people feel good, though these goals may be important and desirable. To gain the level of support needed for successful implementation, EI must be viewed as something that makes good business sense.

The ECT was a direct response to a business need. Only 28 percent of the clients who should have been buying life insurance based on their financial plans were actually doing so. When traditional marketing approaches did not make a significant difference, many people in the company thought that they needed to try something new. Finally, a marketing study showed that emotional factors were the key to clients' reactions to life insurance and that *it was the selling process, not the product, which was the prime source of the negative feeling.*

This led to the idea that the empathy of the advisors was crucial for developing trust with the client. This conclusion led to another study that focused on the planners. They were asked, "How does selling life insurance make you feel?" The answers made it clear that self-doubt was a major barrier to selling. Emotional intelligence training then was developed and offered as a solution to this business problem.

Outcome research on ECT suggested that it has been successful in meeting this business need. Advisors whose management teams went through the program generated 11 percent more sales revenue during the next 15 months than others did.

The company has estimated that this increase translates into an additional $200 million in sales.

GUIDELINE 4: RECRUIT EMOTIONALLY INTELLIGENT LEADERSHIP

Implementing EI initiatives in organizational settings is often a challenging task. Even with the support of powerful sponsors and good timing, one is likely to encounter much resistance. Success depends on the EI of those who orchestrate the implementation effort.

The individuals who implemented ECT used many social and emotional competencies in securing the necessary support. Mitchell picked four people to work on it initially. One of them, Kate Cannon, was selected specifically because of her emotional intelligence or, as they described it at that time, her "process skills" and honesty. Kate eventually became the team leader and the manager in charge of the program. During the next five years, she continued to oversee its implementation. During that time she had to rely upon many emotional and social competencies.

Three competencies, *self-confidence, self-control,* and *adaptability,* were particularly important for successfully establishing ECT. As one of the original team members said, "You need to be okay with ambiguity and okay with failures to do what we did. You need to be able to learn from failures rather than be thrown off by them." She then acknowledged that Kate possessed these crucial abilities.

A good example of how Kate was able to respond adaptively to failure occurred when the team conducted its first pilot test of the leadership version of the program. It was an unmitigated disaster. When the team gathered to debrief at the end of the program, anxiety and gloom filled the air. Most of the group sat around and blamed the participants and the lack of time to prepare adequately. No one wanted to work on fixing the problem at that point. The external facilitator quit the project and took an extended vacation. In contrast, Kate quickly pulled herself together and spent the next two weeks revising the design. Another team member was able to convince a regional vice president to give the team another chance.

Many other setbacks threatened the program. In addition to encountering much resistance (despite the powerful sponsorship), the team had to deal with internal conflict. There were many times when the team could have given up, and eventually all of the team members except Kate did leave the project. Kate kept going. Her self-confidence and self-control enabled her to overcome adversity and learn from it.

Kate was also unusually *conscientious and reliable.* When the pilot test failed, she spent her whole holiday vacation working to fix it. Also, people always could count on her to tell the truth. Kate was described as very independent and outspoken, which sometimes got her into trouble. For example, at her job interview she said, "Don't hire me if you want me to leave my humanity at the door." Nevertheless, because her bosses knew she was trustworthy, they often gave her difficult and delicate assignments. Kate was particularly conscientious in the way she promoted the EI program. One person we interviewed, who was not a particular supporter of the program, said, "If Kate had to choose between continuing the program or receiving more recognition for herself, she'd choose the program." This high level of conscientiousness and commitment were important for the success of the endeavor.

Kate's *initiative and innovation* also were important for success. She was constantly seeking and finding ways to promote the program within the company. She was tireless in her pursuit of new ideas. Her office shelves were stacked high with notebooks that came from the many workshops and seminars that she had attended on a variety of topics. As one person stated, "She falls in love with ideas. That's what motivates her."

Kate also demonstrated high *achievement drive* in the way she promoted the program. She established high standards for quality and monitored the program closely. For example, during the first year or so, she observed the program nearly every day that it was delivered. After every training session, she met with the trainers and spent countless hours debriefing them to find ways to improve it. If the trainers did not meet her exacting standards, their contracts were terminated.

Kate also demonstrated many social awareness competencies in establishing the program. Particularly important were *empathy* and a *strong service orientation.* She was always sensitive about the need to align the program with other people's business issues and concerns. She described her approach thus: "You need to go where the energy is. You need to see it from others' points of view."

Kate also exhibited considerable *organizational awareness.* One of her teammates described her as "very strategic—she sees connections." A good example of this was the way in which the group reached out to the reengineering task force. They realized that the support of this high-profile, influential group within the company could be invaluable for the EI program.

Virtually all of the people with whom we talked said that the program never would have succeeded without Kate's enthusiasm and commitment. One of her bosses, an individual who was not particularly supportive of the program, said, "Her passion was compelling." She assumed *leadership* and inspired others to follow her lead. Kate herself said, "I'm a servant of the idea." The strength of her leadership and commitment was revealed when, after about three years managing the program, she was moved to a new position with a boss who did not support the program. This boss gave her other responsibilities and discouraged her from continuing to work on the EI program. In fact, for one year her performance rating was reduced because her boss thought she spent too much time on the EI program. Kate kept doing it anyway—in her spare time. That commitment inspired others.

Kate would also score high in *influence.* She was constantly thinking of ways to promote the program and generate support for it. She, along with her teammates, came up with many ways of selling the program. For example, they frequently pointed out that this training was similar to techniques used by professional athletes. They even looked for and found a sports psychologist to be one of the first trainers. When they researched the role of emotion in the selling process, they arranged to present it to many different groups within the company. In fact, they looked for every possible opportunity to do so.

The team members spent much time thinking about how to present the results in ways that would reduce resistance. They realized that they needed to link the program to the primary business concerns of selling and making money. They also were sensitive to the process; they decided that rather than presenting the research findings with a hard sell for the program, it would be better to let their audience "come to the conclusions by themselves." For example, the vice president in charge of the top region in the country was a strong supporter of the program. Kate arranged for a video to be made in which he talked about how important EI is for success. The video was played every time the program was offered to groups of financial advisors until the team came up with an even more effective way of selling the idea to participants: Have them come up with their own reasons why EI is important for success.

Collaboration also was important in gaining support for the program. The team reached out to the reengineering task force, and eventually the two groups collaborated on a study that was important in establishing the need for the EI training. This collaboration also helped make EI part of the company's competence model, a major product of the reengineering project. Eventually, a member of the reengineering task force joined the

EI group. Another example of how the team constantly looked for ways to collaborate with others occurred when the team enlisted two of the top sales people in the company to help plan the new program. These individuals became strong advocates of emotional competence training, which further enhanced the credibility of EI in the company.

Although it offered many advantages, the program encountered much resistance and conflict throughout its history. Fortunately, Kate was particularly competent in *dealing with conflict*. She had sought out training in conflict resolution earlier in her career, and she applied what she had learned. In talking about how she dealt with resistance, she described how she looked for "common ground" and "win-win solutions." For example, their approach initially seemed to be incompatible with the views of Doug Lennick, the executive vice president for sales. Instead of fighting or giving up, Kate bought Lennick's book on the importance of emotions and motivation in sales and read it. She found that many similarities existed between the team's approach and Lennick's way of thinking. The team then framed their program more in terms of Lennick's work, and he became a powerful sponsor of the program.

One other competency that proved to be important in this effort was *team capability*. Kate was included in the original team because she was viewed as someone who possessed this competency, and she lived up to her reputation. One member of the team remembered that she was "phenomenal in dealing with process and in helping people make sense of information and make decisions." She was good at keeping the group on task, and, at the same time, she was very supportive of other people. She also was fair: One team member said, "She never let personal issues affect her as a team member."

Kate was not perfect, though. She made some mistakes. Her concern for quality sometimes led her to micromanage. Her independence and outspokenness got her into trouble more than once. On occasion, her commitment and passion for the idea became a liability rather than an asset. Despite Kate's occasional missteps, the program benefited greatly from the many social and emotional competencies that Kate brought to it (table 5-1).

Table 5-1. Social and emotional competencies demonstrated by Kate while implementing ECT.

- Self-confidence: A strong sense of one's self-worth and capabilities
- Adaptability: Flexibility in handling change
- Self-Control: Keeping disruptive emotions and impulses in check
- Conscientiousness and Reliability: Taking responsibility for personal performance; maintaining standards of honesty and integrity
- Initiative and Innovation: Readiness to act on opportunities; being comfortable with novel ideas, approaches, and new information
- Achievement Orientation: Striving to improve or meet a standard of excellence; persistence in pursuing goals despite obstacles and setbacks
- Empathy: Sensing others' feelings and perspectives and taking an active interest in their concerns
- Service Orientation: Anticipating, recognizing, and meeting customers' needs
- Organizational Awareness: Reading a group's emotional currents and power relationships
- Leadership: Inspiring and guiding individuals and groups; aligning with the goals of the group or organization
- Influence: Wielding effective tactics for persuasion
- Change Catalyst: Initiating or managing change
- Communication: Listening openly and sending convincing messages
- Conflict Management: Negotiating and resolving disagreements
- Collaboration and Building Bonds: Working with others toward shared goals; nurturing instrumental relationships
- Team Capabilities: Creating group synergy to pursue collective goals

---

GUIDELINE 5: GIVE THE INITIATIVE PLENTY OF AUTONOMY

Developing emotional intelligence is an innovative and unconventional idea in the organizational world. As such, rigid bureaucracies can easily smother EI initiatives. For EI training to flourish, it must be developed in a setting with a great deal of autonomy and a nonbureaucratic mode of operation. Ideally, it should be developed and initially operated by a self-managed team that has carte blanche to innovate. The team should operate informally with more flexible roles and open flows of information. It also should be kept relatively free of creativity killers, such as surveillance, evaluation, micromanagement, and arbitrary deadlines (Amabile 1988). A particularly good way of achieving this type of setting is to establish a "skunkworks," which was the name of the famed research and development team at Lockheed Martin that sequestered itself and produced a number of innovations.

Skunkworks was the model for the team that developed ECT. When setting up the team, Jim Mitchell, the first sponsor, selected four people whom he judged to be risk takers. He told them they had six months and half a million dollars to figure out why clients were not buying more life insurance. Their mandate did not stop there. He told them to be creative and innovative even if they failed. "It's okay to strike out so long as you learn something," was the way he put it. The written charter for the team included the following language: "The team should bat for a home run every time even if it means we're 0 for 27 at the end. No bunting! To play it safe, to manufacture a nonbreakthrough result just for the sake of saying that we accomplished something concrete will not be acceptable."

Although the team members brought different kinds of expertise and experience, initially the team functioned without a leader and without defined roles. The team's first activity was to hire a consulting firm that specialized in creativity training to organize and lead a retreat for them and a few other employees at the company.

The skunkworks mechanism was crucial for the success of the program. Several people said that they did not think something as innovative as EI training would have emerged from an existing traditional group in the organization. In addition to the autonomy and the mandate to be creative, time was an important aspect of the skunkworks setup. The original charter was extended after six months; the team eventually had almost two years and more than a million dollars to incubate the program. Without so much time for learning, reflection, and experimentation, the team probably could not have been as successful.

The skunkworks project, however, had a downside. During much of its existence, internal tension and conflict plagued the group. Part of the problem was that one person was designated the group's "administrator," while another was put on the team because of her "process skills." Yet no one was supposed to be the "leader." Not surprisingly both of these individuals exerted strong influence and occasionally clashed. In addition to the lack of structure and clear authority within the team, only one person had been selected explicitly because of her social and emotional competence. Some other members of the team seemed to lack important personal and interpersonal competencies that could have helped the team deal more effectively with internal tension.

Despite these problems, the team ultimately succeeded. In general, the high degree of autonomy and lack of structure proved to be assets during the early part of the process when research and innovation were the central tasks. These qualities became liabilities when the group shifted its focus and began to design and deliver programs. At that point, the group needed a more traditional structure. Fortunately, as members of the original team left and were replaced, a more viable structure evolved, with one individual—Kate—emerging as the clear leader.

Organizations do not need to make a large investment in a skunkworks process to provide sufficient autonomy for an EI initiative. In another, smaller company, the program was initiated and developed by the director of training who had a great deal of autonomy in general and reported directly to the president. In this case, it was an individual, not a whole team, who had the autonomy necessary to make the program effective.

GUIDELINE 6: USE RESEARCH

Emotional intelligence activities that are not based on solid research are highly vulnerable. Emotional intelligence training, more so than with other types of activity, must be research-driven. The research should be extensive enough to give decision makers confidence that EI training is based on sound, objective analysis.

For ECT, one expectation was clear from the start: The program was to be based on sound research. The skunkworks participants had been told that, succeed or fail, they should "learn something." One of the few criteria for deliverables was that "decisions must be supported by research." Consequently, one of the first actions taken by the team was to hire a consulting firm to study how emotions entered into the process of buying and selling life insurance. After an initial study that focused on the emotions stirred up for the clients, the firm did a study focusing on the emotions of the financial advisors as they tried to sell life insurance. To confirm these results, the team proposed another study in which they looked at the correlation between advisor success and coping ability. When the results suggested that successful advisors were, in fact, more adept at coping with the emotional side of selling, the team did one more study: They set up an experimental training program to teach advisors how to cope better. Then they checked whether those who went through the program subsequently sold more insurance than a control group.

A number of persons confirmed that these studies were important in helping to make the case for EI training. One person said that he initially was very skeptical about the whole idea, but when he saw the results of the research, "It was startling." As results became available, the team made numerous presentations to different groups in the company. The results had additional credibility because the studies had been conducted by outside experts with academic credentials.

Not all the research, however, was equally compelling. The first two studies were not especially convincing for many people in the company. Fortunately, the results were strong enough for the team to get continued support for more research and development work. Eventually, the team was able to provide convincing sales data, and that made the biggest impression.

Even hard sales data did not convince everyone. Others in the organization were more influenced by qualitative data that struck a "value nerve." For example, it deeply troubled some executives to hear such statements from the advisors' study as, "I feel like a used-car salesman when I try to sell life insurance," or, "It makes me feel unethical." Therefore, hard data on sales, along with emotionally gripping anecdotes, had the biggest effect.

Although the research was important, it did not convince everyone. One person we interviewed claimed, "The evaluation data hasn't been persuasive at all. Everyone knows you can make data say what you want. The data was looked at with suspicion." For this individual and some others, it was more important that the program had the backing of powerful sponsors and that so many participants liked it. Nevertheless, many people in the company were impressed that the program was based on a body of solid research.

GUIDELINE 7: MAINTAIN HIGH QUALITY

Because EI training is not a traditional business concern, it is vulnerable to criticism. To counteract the detrimental effects of such criticism, it is important to ensure that training efforts meet the highest standards; the program must be beyond reproach. If an EI program becomes associated with shoddy, superficial work, resistance will increase further. Opponents of such training need few excuses to kill it.

Kate was concerned about the program's quality from the beginning. She was constantly on the lookout for vulnerabilities to criticism. For this reason, she monitored the trainers very closely, and she fired more than one because they did not meet her exacting standards. She insisted on doctoral-level psychologists because she believed that they would bring a certain level of quality. During the year following the pilot program, Kate and another member of the team sat in on every presentation of the program, even though it meant traveling all over the country and spending at least 30 days just observing the program's delivery. After each delivery, they would spend several hours debriefing the trainers. Although this kind of close monitoring was expensive, Kate believed it was necessary.

GUIDELINE 8: INFUSE EI TRAINING THROUGHOUT ORGANIZATION

To bring EI training into the mainstream, it is useful to find different ways of positioning and presenting it in the organization. For example, different versions of a program can be developed for different groups. Multiple infusion helps to normalize and generalize the concept throughout the organization. It also creates a culture in which people are repeatedly reminded of what they have learned and, thus, are more likely to apply it on the job.

Initially, ECT was designed for financial advisors. After the pilot program, the team proposed that a different version be developed for regional management groups. The rationale was that because the regional managers met weekly with the advisors, they could use this time to reinforce EI lessons if they themselves had been exposed to the training. Eventually, two different versions of ECT evolved for advisors—one for new advisors that became a regular part of the new advisor training program and another for veteran advisors. Somewhat later, yet another version of the program was developed for new managers. It, too, became a regular part of the training for this group. The next version to be developed was targeted at corporate-office management teams. Finally, a version of the program was developed for sales consultants. These were individuals who provided technical assistance to advisors on a variety of matters. Kate was able to convince the head of this group that many of the situations they discussed with advisors had a large EI component. By training the sales consultants to become "emotional coaches," the company could greatly increase their usefulness to the advisors.

In addition to developing several different versions of the program, Kate found other ways to infuse EI into the company. For example, when she was assigned to a high-profile succession planning effort for the company's top executive positions, she found ways to "sneak" EI into the process. Without these multiple infusions of EI into the company, it is unlikely that EI training would have become established and accepted.

CONCLUSION

The eight guidelines presented in this chapter are not unique to EI work. They probably would help to secure organizational support for any new HRD effort. Emotional intelligence, however, is a particularly new and unconventional idea in the world of work. Even though a growing number of managers are recognizing the importance of social and emotional competence for superior performance, many people remain skeptical. Even more managers question whether training and development efforts can actually help people become more emotionally competent. Such efforts are likely to meet considerable resistance. These guidelines can help reduce that resistance.

Which brings up one final point: Resistance is not inherently bad. According to Scott (2000), "Resistance is a sign of change and offers potential for learning." Those who resist may be guided by their own agendas, but, most likely, they also are telling us something valuable. Those who see resistance not as a nuisance but rather as an opportunity to learn and adapt ultimately will be more successful.

ASSESSMENT QUESTIONS

As you move through the process of developing new, more effective social and emotional learning in your organization, ask yourself these questions to gauge how well you have applied the eight guidelines for securing organizational support.

1. Is the timing right for introducing training and development in EI? If not, what needs to change?

2. Is there an influential executive who can provide sponsorship for the initiative?

3. What are the most pressing business needs of the organization at this time? How can promoting EI be linked to one or more of these needs?

4. Who in the organization has the emotional and social competencies necessary for effectively guiding the implementation effort?

5. Will the program be developed by an individual or group with a high degree of autonomy and ample time and resources?

6. How can research be used to develop the program and put it on a solid footing?

7. What needs to be done to make sure that the program's quality is so high that it is beyond reproach?

8. How can EI be infused in different parts of the organization?

Phase 2: Prepare for Change

When organizational support is in place for establishing EI training and the decision has been made to help people become more socially and emotionally competent, determine which competencies are needed to help people become better performers. Then generate in the learners the motivation necessary for change. Phase 2 of the model for developing and implementing EI training initiatives addresses these important tasks through guidelines 9–14.

GUIDELINE 9: ASSESS ORGANIZATIONAL NEEDS

Good training begins with a needs assessment, a step that too many organizations skip. In a survey of companies, for example, only about one in four said they had ways to determine the training needs of their managers (Saari et al. 1988). Use a valid

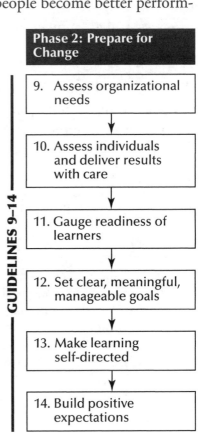

Phase 2: Prepare for Change

9. Assess organizational needs

10. Assess individuals and deliver results with care

11. Gauge readiness of learners

12. Set clear, meaningful, manageable goals

13. Make learning self-directed

14. Build positive expectations

GUIDELINES 9–14

method, and ensure that the desired competencies are congruent with the organization's culture and overall strategy.

For EI training, the needs assessment should indicate which competencies are most important for superior performance in any type of job in the organization. Because many people in the organization may be skeptical about the link between EI and the bottom line, a systematic, rigorous study can be helpful by showing that such a link exists. The needs assessment also should collect the kind of data necessary to show that a gap exists—that learners currently lack the desired particular social or emotional competency. The needs assessment not only suggests what should be the focus for training efforts, but it also serves as a basis for learner motivation. Learners are more motivated if they believe that what they are to learn will pay off in terms of improved performance and attainment of personal and business goals.

When assessing needs it is important to take into account the organization's overall strategy. Different strategies will point to the need for different kinds of competencies. When a training program targets competencies that are viewed as strategic, the organizational environment will be encouraging of the EI orientation, and learners will find the learning to be more meaningful.

Assessing the Organizational Need for a Stress Management Program

Monroy et al. (1997) describe how linking initial research of stress management to organizational needs helped put a stress management initiative at Corning on a strong footing. The initiative began with an assessment of the level of stress within the organization. The program planners injected a question about stress into the periodic climate survey: "During the last two weeks, would you say that you experienced a lot of stress, a moderate amount of stress, relatively little stress, almost no stress at all?" This question was taken from a special supplement of the 1985 National Health Interview Survey, and, thus, Corning's results could be compared to over 16,000 working adults in the United States. The comparison showed that, among Corning's trial sample of several hundred employees, 38 percent answered "a lot of stress," compared to the national sample of 23 percent.

Because Corning was concerned with nonproductive stress, as opposed simply to general stress, the company incorporated two more questions into the survey. One dealt with how well employees were dealing with stress in their organization (that is, coping with stress), and the other addressed the degree to which employees felt they could maintain healthy balances between their work and home lives. The latter question was born of a company initiative being implemented at the time to enhance the quality of people's work lives.

Data analysis showed that employees who reported the highest level of stress were three to four times more likely to view their work groups, organization, and job-related training as ineffective. They did not feel valued as employees. They tended to be dissatisfied with their jobs, and they were more likely to leave the company within the next five years. Overall, the results suggested that by reducing organizational stress and improving the worker's coping abilities, Corning could improve organizational effectiveness and yield benefits in terms of employee health and well-being.

One challenge in applying this guideline is being sure that all of the particular competencies important for success are identified. It is easy to overlook some crucial ones. An example came from the work done at a large airline. Because airlines operate under similar price structures, a competitive advantage can be gained by treating passengers well. Because of this strategic assessment, the way in which flight attendants handled passengers became the focus for training efforts. Initial research suggested that superior performers had two types of competencies: self-management (especially adaptability) and social skills (communication, conflict management, and so forth). A close look at the interaction between an attendant and a disgruntled passenger pointed to two other competencies that were critical: self-awareness and empathy. Self-awareness was important because superior flight attendants were able to identify potential problems at an early stage. They could avoid feeling overwhelmed by the problems if they were aware of their own emotional reactions. Their own feelings, in other words, were early warning signs that helped them to intervene more effectively. Empathy was vital because it helped superior performers retain a positive, sympathetic view of passengers even if the passengers were rude and obnoxious. That sympathy prevented the attendants from becoming overwhelmed by feelings of hostility and anger towards the passengers. Empathy also enabled superior performers to anticipate situations likely to upset passengers and to intervene in ways that would address the problems. In this example, only by carefully assessing the work situation and understanding the nature of EI, were program planners able to identify subtle competencies that led to superior performance.

A number of different assessment methods can provide valid and useful information about which competencies are important for meeting personal and business goals. An especially good approach is to compare superior performers and average performers (Spencer and Spencer 1993). In addition to pinpointing the competencies that contribute most to the bottom line, this approach provides a particularly good basis for motivation because executives are likely to support programs that help employees emulate star performers.

Assessing the Organizational Need for a Caregiver Support Program

This model training program for staff working in group homes began with an extensive study of their needs. To better understand those needs, the program planners "interviewed employees at all levels of the Michigan mental health system..." In the interviews, the planners asked about "both the rewarding and stressful aspects of operating and staffing homes" (Davis-Sacks, Weine, and Heaney 1988).

The program planners also sponsored a conference attended by 60 community and residential care administrators and providers. The conference served as an opportunity for those working in the mental health system to share and discuss their challenges, problems, and concerns regarding community residential care.

These assessment activities suggested that much of the stress of working in a group home did not stem primarily from clients. The main sources of stress came from lack of support and uncooperative relationships among employees and among various actors in the mental health system. Also contributing to stress was a lack of respect from the wider community and the lack of rewards. Although the group home employees received training in skills necessary to do their jobs, they were not provided with training in the competencies needed "to create a strong caregiving team" (Davis-Sacks, Weine, and Heaney 1988).

Based on these findings, the planners designed a program that taught the participants how to develop better social support networks. The program also taught them how to improve team functioning by solving problems as a group.

Useful data can come from a variety of sources. In fact, the best assessments use many different approaches. One way *not* to assess competence needs is to merely ask people what they think the needs are. Even star performers may not realize the qualities that actually make them superior. All too often when companies want to assess competence, they simply ask people whom they regard as experts or people in the position what the ingredients of successful performance might be for that particular job. Then they use those lists to evaluate job applicants or design training.

Assessing Organizational Need for an EI Training Program

The Emotional Competence program at American Express Financial Advisors evolved from a strategic initiative defined by an executive vice president. He wanted to find ways to encourage clients to buy more life insurance. Three different research studies provided increasingly compelling data that such an objective depended on the advisor's ability to cope with the emotions stirred up by selling life insurance in the context of financial planning. Initially, there was considerable skepticism about the value of training in emotional competence. This skepticism diminished when executives saw the results of a study showing that financial advisors who coped better with the emotional aspects of work with clients sold more life insurance. Once they saw the connection between this particular emotional competence and the bottom line, they encouraged advisors and their managers to participate in an EI training program.

In assessing the organizational need, both quantitative and qualitative data proved to be equally valuable. Quantitative data demonstrating a relationship between certain emotional competencies and sales revenues were particularly compelling, but equally useful were vivid anecdotes and quotes from interviews with advisors highlighting why and how those competencies contributed to higher revenues.

GUIDELINE 10: ASSESS INDIVIDUALS AND DELIVER RESULTS WITH CARE

The data should come from multiple sources using several methods to maximize credibility and validity. Deliver the results to the individual with care; be accurate and clear. Also, allow plenty of time for the person to digest and integrate the information. Deliver the results in a safe and supportive environment to minimize resistance and defensiveness. On the other hand, avoid making excuses or downplaying the seriousness of deficiencies.

Like many other guidelines, this one is useful for all types of training and development, but it is particularly important to help people develop greater social and emotional competence. In technical areas, people usually are more aware of their deficiencies and less conflicted about them. For instance, people who never have learned a particular word-processing program likely will be aware that this is a weakness (assuming it is needed to perform well in their job).

People are usually less aware of specific skill weaknesses in the social and emotional domains. People may realize, for example, that they have difficulty in the interpersonal aspects of jobs involving leadership of work groups. They may even know that dealing with difficult employees is a particularly troublesome aspect of their jobs. Similarly, they may recognize that when it comes to stress, they do not always handle it as well as they would like.

It is unlikely, however, that the learners will be able to pinpoint the array of emotional skills they need to develop to improve their functioning in these areas. They are probably even less aware of the underlying attitudes and ways of thinking that get them into trouble or how those ways of thinking trigger complex emotional response patterns that impede their effectiveness in managing stress or dealing with difficult employees. One study (Davis and Kraus 1997) even showed that no correlation exists between people's estimates of their empathy and their scores on objective tests of empathy.

Because these competencies are manifested primarily in social interaction, the best approach to assessment usually involves ratings by those who interact with the person. However, the beliefs, motives, and feelings of the rater influence ratings of social and emotional competence. The boss's view of a manager's self-awareness or ability to empathize may be very different from the view of the manager's peers and subordinates. The best assessment approach for initiating social and emotional learning, therefore, is usually based on multiple ratings conducted from multiple perspectives, such as 360-degree assessments that include boss, peer, and subordinate ratings (Spencer, McClelland, and Kelner 1997).

Industry regularly uses 360-degree feedback for a variety of purposes, and organizations vary in how well they use this tool. When not managed well, it can create resistance rather than readiness. In the most effective development programs, the participants are helped through the review of these ratings, and then they use them to identify the competencies that should be the focus of training efforts.

Nevertheless, even when done well, 360-degree assessment by itself is not always the best approach. An important function of this personal assessment is to build motivation on the part of the learners, and the motivating force depends on the learners' faith in the assessment method (Noe and Schmitt 1986). Therefore, a given assessment method is more motivating for some learners than others. For some individuals, a score on an objective test that they have heard about will be more convincing than the data that emerge from a 360-degree assessment. For this reason, it is best to use several assessment methods.

Motivation for change is further enhanced by the way in which people are given the results of the assessment. In general, feedback is a powerful instigator of change. One study (Kolb, Winter, and Berlew 1968) found that people in self-analytical groups changed more when they received more feedback from other group members. However, feedback is not always helpful. One study found that over one-third of feedback interventions actually decreased performance (Kluger and DeNisi 1996). The way in which people respond to feedback depends on the credibility of the source, the perceived usefulness and accuracy of the message, and the level of detail in the information that is provided (Ilgen, Fisher, and Taylor 1979).

In social and emotional learning, particular sensitivity is required when delivering the results of personal assessments. Because candid feedback—seeing one's self through the eyes of others—can strike to the heart of cherished beliefs about one's self, it must be delivered with great care, in a way that will not trigger defensiveness or denial. Because no evaluation is 100 percent accurate, and because performance feedback is so emotionally potent to people, feedback should serve mainly as a means to open a conversation with people about their own needs for development. That dialogue demands great sensitivity and an atmosphere of safety. In other words, the results need to be delivered with emotional intelligence.

On the other hand, those in a position to provide feedback need to be wary of becoming enablers who tacitly collude with a person's denial of the need to improve (Prochaska, Norcross, and DiClemente 1994). The collusion can be as simple as avoiding the difficult topics, making excuses for them, or otherwise softening the adverse consequences. It is more helpful to talk to people about their specific lapses, making clear how the lapses affect themselves and others; for example, disrupting or undermining the work of a group. The discussion can then move to suggestions about how they might go about building up the necessary emotional competencies. If a person does not respond, the message can be driven home by seeing that each incident of incompetence brings feedback in its wake. Finally, the most helpful mode is to be direct and frequent—though friendly and supportive—when recommending that they work on upgrading their emotional competence.

The motivational effect of delivering assessment results also can be enhanced when learners are helped to identify the specific steps they can take to improve. Individuals who are merely given the results may not know how to redirect their efforts to improve (Korsgaard and Diddams 1996).

Personal Assessment in a Graduate Program

In the master's of business administration (M.B.A.) program at the Weatherhead School of Management, all entering students take a course entitled Managerial Assessment and Development (Boyatzis, Cowen, and Kolb 1995). During the first two or three weeks of the course, they complete a number of exercises and tests, including the learning skills profile, a critical incidents interview, a group discussion exercise, an oral presentation exercise, and a self-assessment questionnaire. The students also complete a learning style inventory, an adaptive style inventory, a technology applications questionnaire, and a personal orientation questionnaire that measures values.

The learning skills profile is a card-sort in which the students are asked to describe themselves by sorting 72 statements of skills into various categories reflecting different levels of skill acquisition. The critical incidents interview is a one-hour interview during which the students are asked to recall and describe in depth three to five recent events in which they felt effective or ineffective at work or during school projects and internships. The students are videotaped while doing the oral presentation and group discussion exercises.

The next seven weeks of the course are devoted to feedback and reflection on the assessment data. The instructors seek to help the students gain a consensus among three internal "voices." The first is the student's own voice: "What do I think my skill level is for each ability?" The second is the voice of others: "What do others think my skill level is for each ability?" The third is the voice of the assessment instruments: "What does my performance on this instrument say about my current ability?" The instructors ask the students to address and discuss where and why significant inconsistencies exist among the three voices.

The students then spend the remaining five weeks of the course developing personal learning plans. These plans guide their learning for the next two years.

The motivational and emotional effect of delivering results also depends upon the context. In social and emotional learning, it is especially important that feedback occur in an atmosphere of safety. When, for example, assessment is used for appraisal purposes, and one's supervisor delivers the results, the effect can be negative. Conversely, if the assessment is used for development purposes and the person giving the feedback is viewed as a disinterested individual whose motivation is to help, then the consequences tend to be much more positive (Kolb and Boyatzis 1970).

Personal Assessment and Feedback in Achievement Motivation Training

This weeklong residential program began with a rather unusual personal assessment. The participants learned how achievement motivation can be measured with thematic apperception test (TAT) stories. Then they learned how to score stories for achievement motivation by practicing on some stories that the instructors distributed to them. Once the participants learned how to score the TAT, they were given stories that they had written before the program began. After scoring the stories, each participant met with a faculty member in a private conference to discuss the stories and scoring. This process for assessment and feedback helped the participants develop greater awareness and insight into their own motivation for achievement. It also challenged them to acknowledge their strengths and weaknesses and to reflect on their ideal self-image. Finally, it encouraged the participants "to relate achievement motivation to events in their everyday business experience" (Aronoff and Litwin 1971).

The amount of time allowed for assimilating the results of assessments is also important. For feedback to be useful and motivating, the individual needs sufficient time to think about the data and its implications. People need more than just an hour or two to study the results of intensive assessment.

Personal Assessment and Feedback in an Executive Coaching Program

The individual coaching for effectiveness (ICE) program begins with an assessment of the individual's strengths, weaknesses, and goals, followed by in-depth feedback and discussion between the coach and the participant. The specific data sources vary depending on the needs of both the individual and the organization. Possible assessment tools include psychometric testing, interviews, work samples, simulations, role play, and 360-degree feedback. Organizers of the program talk with those individuals who request coaching—both the individual who will receive the coaching and their organizational sponsors—to gain a better understanding and decide which methods would be most appropriate.

After the data is collected, it is organized into a format known as GAPS—goals, abilities, perceptions, and standards. Information regarding the person's goals is collected through career interest inventories, written personal statements, value clarification exercises, and personal reflection. Information on abilities is ascertained through professional assessments, observation, feedback, and performance evaluations. The perceptions of others can be obtained through 360-degree feedback surveys and third-party interviews. Information on organizational standards and expectations may come from the organization's leaders, statements of corporate vision and strategy, competency models, job descriptions, performance evaluations, and statements of team goals (Peterson 1993).

In providing feedback to the client, the coach stresses that the information is data, rather than a judgment of the client's capabilities. The coaches strive to help the client understand what the assessments say and try to remain neutral about the meaning of them. For example, a coach might say, "Here is the data about what people said about you. Now, how do you want to make sense of this? What do you want to do with this information?" The coaches see themselves as guides through the process of deciphering the information; they are not definitive authorities. This approach creates a safe atmosphere, which helps the clients avoid the kind of defensiveness that interferes with learning and change.

One approach to providing assessment results that appears to be particularly useful for enhancing motivation for social and emotional learning is "motivational interviewing" (Miller and Rollnick 1991). This technique is an effective method to prepare people for change in a variety of different contexts. Designed to help people recognize and deal with problem behaviors, the technique involves several elements. First, express empathy and understanding without judging, criticizing, or blaming. Second, help the learner recognize the gap between present behavior and the desired behavior. Third, avoid argumentation and confrontation, which are likely to increase resistance and defensiveness. Fourth, bolster self-efficacy during the interview by showing the trainee a path toward change and giving the trainee ownership over the change process. Motivational interviewing techniques, if delivered by competent personnel, can provide the kind of safe atmosphere that is most likely to motivate people to engage in social and emotional learning.

Personal Assessment and Feedback in a Management Development Program

The LeaderLab program goes to great lengths to assess individuals on many levels. Every participant, before beginning the official training portion of the program, must take several different instruments that help elucidate the nature of an individual's strengths, weaknesses, learning style, and goals. One of the first assessment tools is the situational audit, which attempts to clarify one's sense of purpose. This qualitative questionnaire asks participants to describe their sense of purpose as an individual, team or group leader, and as a member of the organization.

At the end of the audit, participants respond to this question: "What are the issues in your leadership situation that you need to address so that you can be more effective in your role?" The next step is to rank the top 10 issues with which they struggle.

LeaderLab also uses a benchmarking questionnaire that examines leadership skills and perspectives, problems that can stall one's career, and challenging assignments. Insights are sought into the strengths and weaknesses associated with each area.

A success style profile (SSP) attempts to discern one's thinking and learning styles (similar to the Myers-Briggs assessment). The Jones inventory of barriers looks at one's values, perceptions, self-image, and perceptions of both the self and others. It tries to pinpoint where the participant stands on certain issues and any barriers to learning that may hold the person back. LeaderLab uses a unique assessment tool, Firo-B Feedback, which is based on feedback from family and friends instead of feedback from work.

Other individual assessment tools include 360-degree feedback and a personal biography, which elicits the participants' insight into major events in their learning. Leaderquest, LeaderLab's own instrument, looks at the individuals' sense of purpose, how they learn, how they deal with people, flexibility, and interpersonal issues.

Each participant is assigned a PA who serves as coach, counselor, advisor, listener, and expert in the process. The PA receives the participant's assessment results prior to the first session in the program and shares individual feedback with the participant in a one-on-one meeting. The goal of these feedback sessions is to help the participant understand what he or she can do with this data so that appropriate action plans can be created and implemented. To help the participants assimilate the results of the assessment and feedback, they also receive a learning log and personal data organizer.

LeaderLab believes that an initial step in understanding one's feedback is to apply the "what?" "so what?" "now what?" analysis. The "what?" refers to the individual's basic understanding of the information. "So what?" alludes to the client's feelings about the feedback. "Now what?" deals with the steps that need to be taken to make any appropriate changes (Young and Dixon 1996).

GUIDELINE 11: GAUGE READINESS OF LEARNERS

After people receive the results of their assessments, they have reached a crucial decision point. Should they embark on a potentially difficult and frustrating effort to improve one or more competencies? Is it worth the price? If the answer to these questions is no, they are not ready to proceed. Unfortunately, in most development efforts, the trainers never consider whether the individual is truly ready to embark on the change effort. Before training commences, the trainers need to gauge the learners' readiness. Do not begin training and development until the learners are ready.

Research on behavioral change programs has suggested that, in general, only about 20 percent of those who enter a program are truly motivated to change (Prochaska, Norcross, and DiClemente 1994). People go through several stages of readiness before they are ready to make a true commitment to change. In the first stage, people deny that they need to change. In the next stage, people engage only in contemplation. They see a need to improve and they are willing to think about it, but they are ambivalent and tend to put off making a decision. Preparation is the focus of the third stage: The individual recognizes that a problem exists and that there are ways of dealing with it. Only at this third stage is the individual ready to sit down and make a specific, concrete plan. The fourth stage occurs when the person acts on the plan (Prochaska, Norcross, and DiClemente 1994).

Many training programs assume that everyone is at the third stage: motivated, committed, and ready to develop a plan of action. Others recognize that the participants need to be motivated, and they include exercises or inspirational lectures to help motivate them. Very few programs pause to assess whether the participants have entered the third stage of readiness before moving into the training phase. If the participants are not ready, the time, effort, and money spent on development are going to be wasted.

Gauging Readiness for Emotional Competence Training

Whenever a management team requests emotional competence training at American Express Financial Advisors, the program coordinator calls the team leader and spends considerable time discussing with him or her the request. Among other things, the coordinator tries to assess why the team leader believes that this type of development experience would be useful and how committed the team members are likely to be. If it turns out that the team leader wants the training for the wrong reasons, he or she is encouraged to seek other kinds of help.

If the team commits to the training, then the trainer calls each team member before the training begins and explores his or her expectations. In this way, the trainer is able to determine who is ready to commence change, who is contemplating the possibility, and who is actively resisting it.

During the initial stage of the training, the learners engage in exercises designed to heighten their awareness of the emotional competencies that are important for success in their jobs, as well as in their personal lives. If they still are not ready to make a commitment to change, they can continue to participate in the program. No one is forced to change. The emphasis is on exploring whether this type of change is desirable and feasible.

Therefore, before training begins the training staff should assess each participant in terms of the four stages of readiness. Doing so is often quite straightforward. After delivering the results of assessments and helping people identify their strengths and weaknesses, simply ask them what they think about working toward change in some area.

If the response is negative, vague, or ambivalent, then they are not ready. At that point, the best a trainer can do is to help people to explore further their personal values and aspirations, and, perhaps, evaluate the barriers that prevent them from making a commitment to change.

Gauging Readiness in the JOBS Program

The JOBS program focuses on three components to assess a participant's readiness and motivation for change. First, does the participant believe that he or she has a problem to solve? If it is accepted that a problem exists, the next step is to see if the participant possesses the knowledge necessary to solve it. In other words, does the participant hold a vision for possible paths to address the problem? Finally, does the participant have "a general sense of confidence and mastery, a specific self-efficacy to follow their action path successfully?" If a participant seems to be leaning toward a no response to any of these questions, he or she is unlikely to make the necessary efforts to achieve the goals of the program. For those individuals, the support of others plays a pivotal role in helping them to become more ready for change (Vinokur, Price, and Schul 1995).

GUIDELINE 12: SET CLEAR, MEANINGFUL, MANAGEABLE GOALS

Goals should be linked to personal values and broken down into manageable steps. People need to be clear about what the desired competency is, how to acquire it, and how to show it on the job. Spell out the specific behaviors and skills that make up the target competency. Make sure that the goals are specific, meaningful, and optimally challenging.

When Alice in Wonderland asked the Cheshire cat which way she should go, his sage response was, "That depends a good deal on where you *want* to go." Fuzzy goals for self-development leave people as perplexed as Alice. Specific, clear, and measurable goals for change make clear the path ahead and serve as benchmarks of progress along the way. Without such clear goals, people can easily lose their way.

Setting Goals in Achievement Motivation Training

One of the basic themes of achievement motivation training is that it "involves presenting the possibility and desirability of change of personal goals, encourages the participant to commit himself [or herself] to these goals, and institutes the means to maintain this commitment" (Aronoff and Litwin 1971). By the third day of the program, goal setting became a major focus of the training process. The trainers helped the participants consider the demands of their job for achievement-oriented performance, their goals, and the level of achievement motivation revealed in their thematic apperception tests. Then the trainers asked the participants to state publicly "whether they wanted to develop any further degree of achievement motivation and, if so, which aspects or categories they felt would be particularly appropriate" (Aronoff and Litwin 1971). The trainers then encouraged the participants to set concrete goals for a program of achievement motivation development.

Many studies have noted that the process of setting change goals is a powerful motivational tool. For example, in a classic study of the use of goals in training, Kolb, Winter, and Berlew (1968) found that self-directed change was enhanced when the method was modified to emphasize conscious goal setting. In the organizational behavior literature, goal setting has been shown to improve performance across a wide range of domains (Locke and Latham 1990; Wexley and Baldwin 1986).

Goals are not alike. Specific goals are more effective in improving performance than general or vague goals. A general goal, such as "Learn how to listen better to subordinates," is less effective than "Use active listening with subordinates at least three times each day for three weeks" (Bassett and Meyer 1968; Locke and Latham 1990).

Setting Learning Goals for the Weatherhead M.B.A. Program

After several weeks of assessment, feedback, and reflection, the students in Weatherhead's M.B.A. program list their personal and career goals. Then the instructors help them to break the goals into subgoals and action steps. They challenge the students to provide a rationale for each goal and to indicate how they and others will be able to tell when they have accomplished it. Students ultimately must state their goals in terms of an outcome that is specific and concrete, personally meaningful, affirmatively stated, realistic, and tied to a time frame.

For instance, one M.B.A. student lacked the self-confidence to approach people about part-time jobs. The larger goal of developing self-confidence was overwhelming and vague, but he was helped to break it into smaller, more realistic action steps. The first was to update his résumé, a task that was easy for him, because he had no need to approach anyone. The next steps, which were increasingly difficult, were to call the chairman of the finance department during the coming month to request a meeting, meet with the chairman to discuss opportunities, and meet with his mentor, who was a local executive. Finally, he would search the local want ads and call to apply for promising jobs. In this way, the goal of increasing self-confidence became attainable, and the process met with steady progress and success rather than frustration and failure.

Previous assessment activity is used to make sure that the students' goals are linked to personal values. Such exercises as "My Values" help students identify the conditions and forms of conduct that matter most. In career interviews, the students visualize what their desired career will look like in 10 to 20 years, and then the instructors encourage them to consider the relationship between their values and their desired careers.

The creation of a learning plan integrates the students' values with their understanding of their strengths and weaknesses. In the learning plan, the students explain why each goal is important to them and how it relates to their career. The students also identify which competencies are needed to achieve each goal that they set for themselves. In helping the students develop a learning plan, faculty members encourage them to be realistic about how many abilities they can work on improving at one time. They tell the students not to place 10 ability goals on the high-priority list, because it would not be realistic to grow in each of these areas at once.

One other important feature of the learning plan is that it includes a timetable that integrates all the action steps the students will undertake during the subsequent 18-month period (Boyatzis, Cowen, and Kolb 1995).

People will be most motivated to learn and change if they believe that doing so will help them achieve goals that they value. If a change matters little to people, they will not pursue it. Often the most salient personal values are work-related, but they need not be. Trying to motivate learners by showing them that training will contribute to career success will be difficult if success is unimportant to them. Fortunately, other incentives for social and emotional learning are not difficult to find.

Linking Learning Goals to Personal Values

Peterson (1996) describes the ICE program in which coaches attempt to link participants' goals to their personal values through the use of written mission statements, value clarification exercises, career interest instruments, and personal reflection. In one case, a coach spent "a good part of sessions 2 and 3 exploring the client's vision and values, both as a person and as a leader." Between sessions, the client spent more time reflecting on her values and the professional accomplishments that she wished to achieve. Bringing these new insights back to the coaching process "sparked an even more intense passion for her development as a leader."

It also is important to break goals into manageable steps. Trying too much too soon can set people up for failure. For many people, trying to bring about even modest improvements in emotional competence can be frustrating. Although challenging goals are more motivating than simple ones, it is important that the goals be attainable. Modest aspirations make success more likely and so foster a sense of efficacy that gives people the confidence they need to move forward. When people reach a goal, their self-efficacy increases, which leads to the setting of new, more challenging goals (Bandura and Cervone 1983; Hall

1976; Snyder 1993). Breaking the goal down into specific steps—with the first challenges easier than subsequent ones— works best. Too daunting a task or unrealistic a goal is a setup for failure. The best approach is to formulate a workable, step-by-step action plan.

Breaking Goals Into Manageable Steps

The JOBS program incorporates steps that move the participants into increasingly challenging situations. For example, job seekers learn at one point how to conduct networking telephone calls first by watching the trainers model the wrong way to do it. The job seekers then generate ideas and suggestions for better handling the telephone call. The next step requires the clients to perform role plays themselves, incorporating the suggestions made by their peers. Finally, when the job seekers are comfortable handling the telephone call in a role-play situation, they are encouraged to use these new skills and insights in their own job search process outside of the program. Research into how people change their own behavior suggests that public declaration of change goals seems to enhance their motivating properties. For instance, one study (Heatherton and Nichols 1994) found that this kind of public declaration was present in many successful life-change attempts. On the other hand, unsuccessful changers never mentioned making such a public declaration. Once people have formulated learning goals, it is often useful to have them state the goals publicly even if only to one other person.

GUIDELINE 13: MAKE LEARNING SELF-DIRECTED

People are more motivated to change when they freely choose to do so. As much as possible, allow people to decide whether or not they will participate in the development process, and have them set the change goals themselves. Let them continue to take charge of their learning throughout the program, and tailor the training approach to the individual's learning style.

In social and emotional learning, choice is particularly important. Because these competencies are an integral part of each person's self-image and personality, it is better if they are free to choose whether to engage in such training.

It also is important that the choice be real. If trainees are given a choice but not assigned to the training they initially selected, they will be less motivated to learn than those who were given no choice (Baldwin, Magjuka, and Loher 1991; Magjuka, Baldwin, and Loher 1994). Tobin (2000) makes the point that, in fact, all learning must be self-directed: "Although the corporation or an instructional designer has designed the content of a training program to meet specific learning objectives, whether I am in a classroom, reading, or taking a computer-based training program, I, as the learner, decide what is important to me and, therefore, I choose what to learn." The learner may not have control over what is being *taught,* but the learner always has control over what is *learned.*"

Consider what happened when some managers and supervisors at a large high-technology firm were assigned randomly to one of two groups. One group received a memorandum from their supervisor requiring attendance at a training session; the other group received a memorandum from the training department describing the same training program that merely informed the managers when the training would be offered. Those people given a choice to attend had higher motivation to learn, were more satisfied once they went through the training, and mastered the training better than those forced to go (Hicks and Klimoski 1987). Some other excellent ways to demoralize employees who are forced to attend training include telling them it is the only way they can keep their job or that they have to go as "punishment" for doing poorly in their jobs (Quinones 1996).

There is a pitfall, however, to the very common practice of offering people a menu of training programs from which to choose. Some particularly popular courses fill up right away, so people are turned away or offered a second or third choice. One of the perils of choice occurs when people have to settle for a less desirable topic. Such disgruntled trainees, understandably, have very low motivation to attend or to learn, and so learn very little (Baldwin, Magjuka, and Loher 1991). The caveat for organizations: If you promise training, deliver it to those who want it; sending people to something else is likely to be a wasted effort.

In self-directed learning, the learner is in control throughout the change process, and a number of studies suggest that people are more likely to change when they are in control. For instance, in a weight loss program (which involves self-regulation competencies), people who believed they were responsible for their weight loss were more effective in maintaining their weight after the program ended than those who believed the program or their therapist was responsible for weight loss (Sonne and Janoff 1982).

Self-Directed Change in Stress Management Training

In one stress management program, the participants were taught a variety of approaches to relaxation. They were then encouraged to try each one and select the best one for them. If none worked well, they were encouraged to try other approaches to managing stress, such as improving their time management skills. The basic message of the program was that people differ, and no one approach to managing stress will work well for everyone.

Research on the processes that people use for independent change also supports the notion that change is facilitated by self-control. Stories of successful life change attempts, compared to unsuccessful ones, more often involved self-reward and self-reinforcement. The successful changers were more likely to feel that they had control over their behavior and possessed greater self-control in general (Heatherton and Nichols 1994).

Self-Management Training

In this approach to social and emotional change, the learners are put in charge of every stage of the change process. For example, in one program designed for employees who had poor job attendance, the trainers first taught the participants how to set proximal and distal goals for job attendance (Frayne and Latham 1987). The participants then set their own goals. Next, the trainers taught the participants how to write behavioral contracts with themselves for administering reinforcers and punishers that they chose for themselves. The participants also were responsible for administering the incentives for themselves. Finally, the participants had the opportunity to identify potential problems that they might encounter in implementing their plans, and the trainers helped them to develop their own solutions to those problems.

GUIDELINE 14: BUILD POSITIVE EXPECTATIONS

Show learners that social and emotional competence can be improved and that such improvement will lead to valued outcomes. Expectations about performance can become self-fulfilling prophecies (Eden 1990). People who are confident that they can succeed in a training program will tend to be more motivated and, not surprisingly, more successful (Gist, Schwoerer, and Rosen 1989; Ryman and Biersner 1975). Related research on change processes in psychotherapy also suggests that efficacy expectations play an important role in motivation for change. For example, Grencavage and Norcross (1990) reviewed 50 publications on diverse forms of psychotherapy to distill common change factors. They found that the most frequent client characteristic mentioned was "positive expectancies and hope for improvement." Similar findings were reported by Bandura, Adams, and Beyer (1977).

Building Positive Expectations for Change in the JOBS Program

The trainers in the JOBS program help learners develop positive expectations for change in several ways before and during the program. For example, when trainers help the participants develop the emotional and social competencies needed for job interviews, they begin by having the participants observe the trainers engage in a role play of a job interview. During the role play, the trainers intentionally make a number of mistakes. At the conclusion, they ask the learners to identify all the mistakes that they observed and offer suggestions for improvement. After the learners have offered a number of suggestions, the trainers do the role play again, incorporating the participants' suggestions. The participants then see how much better the trainers do using the participants' suggestions. The trainers conclude by pointing out that the participants already know most of what they need to know to be successful in job interviews. The participants realize that being successful in job interviews is not as difficult as they thought and that success is within their reach (Price and Vinokur 1995).

Learners' expectations must be realistic. If learners enter a development activity with unrealistically high expectations, their motivation could be undermined. This idea was demonstrated convincingly in a study that manipulated the expectations of trainees through pretraining memoranda (Hicks and Klimoski 1987). The trainees who received a realistic preview of what the training would involve were more motivated to learn, viewed training as more appropriate, and believed that they profited from the training more than trainees who received a brief, overly positive training notice.

Unfortunately, in the case of social and emotional learning, many people are skeptical that EI can be improved. People who find social and emotional problems challenging will be particularly dubious about *their* ability to improve. To maximize motivation, learners need to believe not only that greater emotional competence will lead to valued outcomes but also that they can improve their emotional competence. Trainers, managers, and co-workers can help learners develop this belief by creating situations in which they successfully engage in such learning or see someone like them do so. Verbal persuasion also is sometimes effective in enhancing self-efficacy beliefs.

Helping Learners Build Positive Expectations in a Stress Management Program

The trainers in the Corning stress management program tried to instill in people a sense of confidence by presenting the techniques in ways that empowered the participants. They delivered the message that the techniques were not overly complex or difficult to learn. They would say, "These are techniques that you have used before. You just may not necessarily have stayed with them or been consistent." In addition, the trainers presented techniques in such a way that the participants could learn a technique well enough to feel competent in a single session. Then they would tell the participants, "You now know an effective technique for helping you to manage stress in your lives. Now it's just a matter of practicing."

On the other hand, the trainers also made sure that participants' expectations for the training were realistic from the outset. During the first session of the program, the trainers initiated a discussion of why people had chosen to participate in the program. If their reasons were to complain about the company, the trainers told them that this was not the purpose of the program. They said very clearly and emphatically, "If you think you are fine, and you are really here because someone else is driving you crazy and you want to get them to change, that is not an appropriate use of the program."

ASSESSMENT QUESTIONS

How effectively does your organization prepare learners to become more emotionally intelligent? Which competencies are needed in your workplace? How can you instill the motivation for change in learners? As you move through the process of developing new, more effective social and emotional learning in your organization, ask yourself these questions to gauge how well you have applied the six guidelines for preparing for change:

1. What steps will you take to assess the need for emotional intelligence training?

2. What competencies are most critical for superior performance in the jobs that are the target of the initiative? What competencies are most critical for the organization's strategy?

3. How will the learners' strengths and limitations on the critical competencies be assessed? How will you ensure that the assessment data will be valid and credible to the learners?

4. Will the results be delivered in a safe environment, and will the learners have sufficient time to make sense of the results?

5. How will you gauge the readiness of the learners before the development process actually begins? What will be done with individuals who are not ready to embark on a change effort?

6. Does each learner have clear change goals? Are the goals personally meaningful and linked to personal values? Are the goals broken down into manageable steps?

7. Is the learning self-directed? To what extent are people able to decide whether to participate in the development process? To what extent are the learners able to set the change goals themselves?

8. How can the learners' learning styles and preferences guide the learning process?

9. How will the trainers show the learners that social and emotional competence can be improved and that improvement will lead to valued outcomes?

7

Phase 3: Train and Develop

Much of the activity during phase 2 was designed to enhance motivation. Motivation continues to be important during this phase, which is concerned with doing the actual work of change. Because social and emotional learning requires substantial investments of time and effort, and because such learning can pose threats to one's self-esteem, trainers must continue to monitor the learners' motivation and intervene, if necessary, to bolster it.

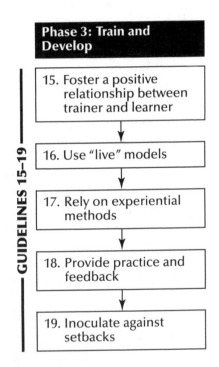

GUIDELINES 15–19

Phase 3: Train and Develop

15. Foster a positive relationship between trainer and learner

16. Use "live" models

17. Rely on experiential methods

18. Provide practice and feedback

19. Inoculate against setbacks

GUIDELINE 15:
FOSTER A POSITIVE RELATIONSHIP BETWEEN TRAINER AND LEARNER

Carefully select trainers based on their warmth, empathy, genuineness, and their ability to relate to the learners. They must also possess technical knowledge of the subject and good presentation skills. Once they begin to do the training, give the trainers ongoing evaluation and feedback on these competencies.

In social and emotional learning, the relationship between the trainer and learner is critically important. For example, in a program designed to teach people to be more assertive, the participants were less likely to drop out and showed more positive change at the end of the program if they had a positive relationship with the trainer (Ford 1978).

Fostering a Positive Relationship Between Learners and Trainers in the Caregiver Support Program

During the first session, the trainers "worked to create a climate of trust, to reinforce the sharing of ideas and feelings among participants, and to establish themselves as credible sources." (Heaney, Price, and Rafferty 1995) Trainers were paired so that their strengths and weaknesses complemented each other. To be perceived as likable and accepting, the trainers provided unconditional positive regard for the participants, gave specific and contingent praise when participants tried to change their behavior, and made moderate self-disclosures about their own attempts at change.

For example, one trainer began the first session by revealing a personal story. He shared with the group how he felt when he was working in a group home and a client committed suicide: "It was real painful for me. But, it was very helpful to me that I could turn to others on the staff to talk through my feelings." By combining moderate self-disclosure with positive role modeling, the trainer connected more deeply with the participants (Heaney, Price, and Rafferty 1995).

Although many factors influence the relationship between trainers and learners, the personal qualities of the trainer are particularly important in social and emotional learning. Several studies have suggested that trainers who are empathic, warm, and genuine—all attributes of EI—develop better relationships with participants in behavioral change programs, and these trainers are the ones who are more likely to be successful (Grencavage and Norcross 1990; Horvath and Symonds 1991). On the other hand, trainers who use a directive-confrontational style only succeed in making participants more resistant (Henry, Schacht, and Strupp 1986; Miller, Benefield, and Tonigan 1993).

In classroom settings, where most research on the link between trainer qualities and training outcomes has been done, studies have shown that specific trainer qualities, such as being "well organized" and having the ability to "answer questions clearly and thoroughly," are important attributes (Goldstein 1993).

In addition, research on behavioral change in other contexts has amply documented this link. For example, in a review of 50 articles on factors associated with change in psychotherapy, Grencavage and Norcross (1990) found that "development of a therapeutic relationship or working alliance" was the most frequently cited factor in successful change. A meta-analysis of 24 studies found an average effect size of $r = 0.26$ for the link between quality of the therapeutic alliance and outcome (Horvath and Symonds 1991).

Why and how does the relationship between trainer and learner help bring about change? Some experts believe that the relationship itself helps bring about the change. More likely, a positive relationship encourages the learner to remain committed to the change process and to engage in the sort of activity necessary for success.

Fostering a Positive Relationship Between the Trainer and Learner in the JOBS Program

The relationship between the trainer and the participants is seen to be an essential component of the JOBS program. The designers of the program believe it is important that the participants feel as though they can relate to the trainers on a personal level. It is particularly important that they feel that the trainers can understand and empathize with their predicaments. For this reason, the program hires trainers who have been unemployed and, as such, can relate to the participants with whom they will be working. Before they are hired, people who want to become trainers must prepare and deliver a lesson "in anything" to a group of JOBS staff members. In evaluating the performance, the staff looks especially at how sensitive and empathic the potential trainer is.

Once they are hired, the trainers go through a rigorous 240 hours of training to learn how to deliver the program. One of the things they learn is how to use moderate self-disclosure to develop trust with the participants in the program. The trainers are encouraged to talk about their own experiences in coping with job loss. The trainers might say something such as, "I was once unemployed myself, and I found that a lot of my friends didn't really understand what being unemployed was like. Although some of them told me I would be okay, I wasn't sure I would make it sometimes. Still, I told myself that I had to keep plugging away. It was persistence that led to success" (Vinokur, Price, and Schul 1995).

This guideline has important implications for the selection of trainers for social and emotional learning efforts. In some of the model programs (chapter 3), the trainers were required to have doctorate degrees in psychology. This, however, was no guarantee that they could develop a positive relationship with program participants. In one program, for example, the coordinator had to fire several psychologists because they approached social and emotional training as though it were psychotherapy. Some of the psychologists also failed because they could not adequately understand and relate to the concerns of individuals working in a business organization. On the other hand, the coordinator of this program continued to use psychologists because she believed that they had the special training necessary to help people deal with some of the strong emotional reactions that can occur during social and emotional learning. She also believed that the psychologists' special status gave them the credibility necessary for some of the participants to accept them as teachers.

In some of the other model programs, people with less formal training, but who had the necessary personal qualities, were selected. These individuals received several weeks of intensive training before they began doing the work, and then they were closely monitored and supervised for some time after that.

Ultimately, the importance of formal, advanced training in psychology or a related field depends on the nature of the development activity. In some situations, nonprofessionals can, with the right kind of training, help people in organizations develop greater social and emotional competence. In certain kinds of training and development activities, advanced training and certification may be highly desirable. In either case, however, the relationship between the teacher and learners is of critical importance when the goal is social and emotional learning.

Whether or not the trainer is licensed or certified, confidentiality is a critical issue in EI-based training. Effective training often requires individuals to think and talk about aspects of themselves that they might not normally discuss with others in their work settings. It is critical that the learning environment be a safe one. To ensure such safety, participants in an EI-development effort must be assured that what they say and do will not become public knowledge.

Fostering a Positive Relationship Between the Trainers and Learners in a Stress Management Program

The trainers in this program typically were psychologists who had 10 years' experience. They enhanced their credibility in the program by talking about real-life examples from their practices. Their willingness to listen to the participants and talk about their concerns also helped build a positive, trusting relationship.

Because the programs were open to all of the employees of Corning, the trainers had to be individuals who could relate to a wide variety of groups. Trainers had to be equally comfortable and effective with hourly factory workers and with top executives from research and development.

It became clear to the program designers that "the more open and human the trainer was, the higher the likelihood that employees would respond positively to the training. The ability of the trainer to challenge participants empathetically to consider new behaviors, to make the training more relevant to the job situation, and to connect work and home life were far more influential than whether the content was systematic relaxation or biofeedback" (Monroy et al. 1997).

GUIDELINE 16: USE "LIVE" MODELS

In learning a new behavior, it is helpful to have access to a living, breathing model—a person who shows, through his or her actions, how the competency appears when applied. To a great extent, social and emotional competence is developed by watching others. One cannot learn to solve quadratic equations just by watching someone else do so, but much can be learned about how to work through a conflict with a co-worker by observing a good model do it. Learning is further enriched when trainers encourage and help learners to study, analyze, and emulate the models. In other words, we become more emotionally intelligent by watching an emotionally intelligent person in action (Bandura 1977; Tannenbaum and Yukl 1992).

Models can be used in a variety of ways in EI training. Trainers can act as live models during a training program. Other participants also can act as live models. Models can be portrayed on videotape. One advantage of videotaped models is that one can often use models that otherwise would not be available. In some training, for example, popular and respected executives serve as models in training videotapes to be used in the organization. Such models can be particularly persuasive for some participants.

For example, modeling was the basis for a new sales training program at Xerox Corporation. Xerox was able to raise the competence of its sales force by setting up a new training program in which new hires observed high performers as they modeled selling behaviors. The program replaced the traditional six-week training at a central location. Not only did the new training boost sales, but turnover among sales representatives fell by 20 percent, and Xerox realized savings of $345,000 annually by eliminating centralized training delivery (Sawyer 1999).

Using Models in Behavior-Modeling Training for Supervisors

Behavior-modeling training relies heavily on models to teach emotional competence. In many versions, the trainers present a positive model on videotape after reviewing with the participants the content to be learned. After the learners view the videotape, they discuss the skills they observed. Each model for handling a difficult interaction typically is broken down into critical steps that produce a sequence of events to be followed when a supervisor interacts with a subordinate. The model interactions are developed in a way that recognizes the differences in the subordinates with whom supervisors typically must deal.

To ensure an early successful experience, the first skill-practice exercise in each module is designed to be quite similar to the model. Developing a high level of skill and facilitating transfer back to the job requires that each subsequent exercise become more difficult and different from the model in the film.

Modeling also occurs during practice sessions. The participants observe, take notes, and discuss four other skill-practice exercises in addition to the one they do themselves. The trainer helps them identify those aspects of their peers' performance that are most worthy of emulation. They also get an opportunity to see how different styles are used effectively to achieve the same results. That way, they can choose models that suit their own style and are easiest for them to emulate.

GUIDELINE 17: RELY ON EXPERIENTIAL METHODS

Emphasize active learning. Spend more time in demonstrations and practice of the competencies than in presenting lectures on them or having learners read about them. Active, concrete, experiential methods, such as role plays, group discussions, and simulations, usually work better than lecturing or assigned reading for social and emotional learning.

To "reprogram" neural circuits connecting the amygdala and neocortex (figure 4-1), people need to engage in the desired pattern of thought, feeling, and action. The neocortex understands words and ideas, but the amygdala does not. The amygdala, one of the centers of emotion, is much older in evolutionary terms than is the neocortex. Learning in the brain's emotional centers occurs not through words and ideas but through simple, repeated actions and vivid experiences. The language of the amygdala is the language of feeling, impulse, and action. For this reason, lectures can increase understanding of EI, but experiential methods usually are necessary for people to behave in a more emotionally intelligent way.

Using Experiential Learning Methods in the LeaderLab Program

LeaderLab uses several unusual experiential learning activities, such as acting, artistic work, and "three-dimensional problem solving." According to the staff responsible for the program, "These activities can be controversial—perceived as uncomfortable and disconnected from the program and therefore a 'GAG' (going against the grain) experience for some participants. However, they can also provide powerful learning experiences for many" (Young and Dixon 1996).

One of the most powerful social and emotional learning activities is three-dimensional problem solving. This exercise involves the expression of emotion in nonverbal ways. "Participants physically represent problems or issues by arranging, or sculpting, the group to demonstrate relationships, communication, and so forth. They then resculpt the group to represent the resolution of the problem. The activity is conducted silently, providing another avenue for nonverbal expression and learning" (Young and Dixon 1996).

LeaderLab also relies on simulations. One simulation entitled World Products International "is a three-hour activity that puts participants into the organizational roles of this fictional company. They must deal with rapid change, capital allocations, diverse groups, and environmental and community issues, and they must wrestle with the values of the various divisions of the corporation, as well as with the values of the individuals involved" (Burnside and Guthrie 1992). This simulation helps the participants develop several important competencies, particularly self-awareness and organizational awareness.

A study of managerial and sales training programs offered in a large corporation demonstrated the superiority of experiential methods for social and emotional learning. The programs that used experiential methods were twice as effective, as measured by ratings of supervisors and peers, for improving performance as other types of programs were. Furthermore, the return on investment for the experiential programs was seven times greater (Spencer, McClelland, and Kelner 1997). In another study, police recruits participated in two types of training designed to teach them how to handle interpersonal conflicts better. One training program relied primarily on lecture methods, whereas the other emphasized experiential methods. The recruits who participated in the experiential alternative did significantly better on the job after training as measured by a variety of performance indicators (Zacker and Bard 1973).

Research on change processes in psychotherapy also has pointed to the superiority of experiential methods. An example was a study of the components of cognitive therapy associated with change. The results suggested that concrete methods predicted positive change in mood; but less focused, more abstract discussions did not (Robins and Hayes 1993). Research in neuroscience has reached similar conclusions, suggesting that emotional learning is more likely to occur when novelty, dramatic retreat settings, and powerful stimuli that engage all the senses mark the experience (Kosslyn and Koenig 1995).

Using Experiential Learning Methods in Achievement Motivation Training

The designers of this program included a number of activities designed to get the participants actively engaged in "achievement thinking." In one activity, the trainers gave the participants pictures depicting ambiguous situations, and the participants wrote imaginative stories about the pictures, which were "deliberately saturated" with many kinds of achievement-oriented thinking. In another activity, the participants did the same with brief descriptions of business situations. "The practice exercises gradually became a competitive game, with each participant having as his [or her] object the working in of more [Need for] Achievement categories than any of the other participants" (Aronoff and Litwin 1971).

Another activity involved a business game designed so that the participant could "try out achievement thinking and achievement-related action and see its effects on his [or her] performance ... The game involves manufacturing a series of products from Tinkertoy parts. Individual scores are derived regarding riskiness of decisions made, use of data from previous stages, planning, and anticipation of difficulties and profitability of new products devised. After the game was played with the group, individual scores were fed back, and these were discussed in relation to the individual's level of achievement motivation and the demands of his [or her] job for achievement-oriented performance" (Aronoff and Litwin 1971) .

Although experiential interventions seem to be especially productive for social and emotional learning, insight also can play a useful role. Insight serves as a natural link between situations, thoughts, and feelings. It enhances self-awareness, the cornerstone of EI. Insight often paves the way for meaningful behavioral change. For example, in a study of those who attempted some kind of life change, the results revealed that one out of five people who successfully made changes "gained new understanding of [his or her] situation through a sudden flash of insight into their behavior." They also were more likely to describe themselves as having discovered "a new sense of self-knowledge and understanding." In contrast, none of those who failed to change expressed any type of insight at all (Heatherton and Nichols 1994). Although insight can play an important role in social and emotional change, the dominant mode of learning should be experiential.

Combining Insight and Experiential Learning in Supervisor Training

The interaction modeling program provides a good example of how a highly experiential approach to developing emotional and social competence integrates insight into the training. In more recent versions of the program, learners analyze a written case study, such as one about a supervisor who must discuss a performance problem with a subordinate. They discuss as a group how best to apply the information and skills they learned in the content overview. This activity helps ensure that the learners develop "an accurate understanding of the skills to be learned" (Pesuric and Byham 1996). After the learners discuss the case study, they view the positive model video. The model is designed to provide an "answer" to the case problem.

GUIDELINE 18: PROVIDE PRACTICE AND FEEDBACK

Encourage learners to practice whenever possible at work and in other life contexts, and help them to continue to practice the new behaviors for several months. The relationship between practice and learning is one of the oldest and best-established principles in psychology. In social and emotional learning, practice is more important, because old, ineffective neural connections need to be weakened and new, more effective ones established. Such a process requires repetition over a prolonged period of time. Learners need to practice on the job, not just in the training situation, for transfer to occur.

Relying on a single seminar or workshop is one of the most common errors made in social and emotional learning programs. Even an intense workshop conducted over several days usually is not sufficient to help people unlearn old, entrenched habits and develop new ones that will persist. The most effective training programs include repeated sessions of practice and feedback. The principles of distributed, rather than massed, practice, and over-learning are well established in the classic literature on learning (Baldwin and Ford 1988; Dempster 1988). Research on "dose-effect" in psychotherapy also shows that the longer people work at changing, the more durable the change will be. Most people do not show stable changes until they have completed a dozen or more sessions (Howard et al. 1986).

The Role of Practice in Interaction Modeling
Training for Supervisors

Practice plays a large role in this interpersonal skill-training program. In six hours of training, approximately four hours are spent in skill practice. The program also uses distributed practice by having one day of training followed by a couple of weeks back on the job, followed by another training session. By alternating training with practice, the trainer can reinforce the new skills while troubleshooting any roadblocks.

Each skill module consists of approximately four skill practices. This allows all the participants to practice handling an interaction in the role of supervisor. They also get to see the situation from the point of view of the employee by playing the role of a subordinate in another situation. "In addition, each supervisor actively observes, takes notes, and discusses four other skill practice exercises" (Pesuric and Byham 1996). The learners are able to internalize the social and emotional skills needed to handle difficult interactions by practicing variations of the interaction in a series of skill-practice exercises, with subsequent exercises becoming more complex and difficult than the previous one. Because training occurs in small groups, participants have plenty of time to practice the skills and receive in-depth coaching and feedback.

After each practice exercise, the learners spend considerable time receiving and giving feedback to one another. During a practice rehearsal, learners who are not playing the role of supervisor or subordinate observe and take notes on the supervisor's use of the action steps. The practice interaction is often videotaped, too. Following the role play, the learners view the videotape and discuss how the action steps were applied. "The focus is on successes rather than difficulties encountered. However, if the learner playing the role of supervisor leaves out or is unable to perform one of the action steps, the trainer conducts a mini-rehearsal on the spot. The person playing the supervisor role is allowed to perfect the skill and demonstrate proficiency before the feedback is completed. Thus, the final outcome for the learners is not an evaluation that implies success or failure but a demonstration that shows their success" (Porras and Anderson 1981).

The learners also use practice sessions to help them address problems in applying the skill on the job. To encourage learners to practice the skills on the job, the trainers ask them at the end of each module to "describe a situation where they can apply the interaction skill on the job" (Pesuric and Byham 1996). After they have had a week or two to apply what they have learned, they return to the training environment and discuss their experiences. If the learned skills did not successfully address an on-the-job situation, the skills are tried again in a skill-practice session to find out why they did not work. Sometimes this leads to greater mastery of the learned skill; other times it suggests an alternative method, which then is practiced several times.

The trainers also ask the participants to create a "critical step card." This laminated plastic card, which the learners take with them, lists and describes the critical steps for the modules they complete. The trainers encourage the participants to make these cards available during challenging interactions so that they will be reminded of the steps that they learned. The cards serve as an easily accessible, helpful reminder of the lessons they learned throughout the training.

Feedback is important during the change process as a way of indicating whether the learner is on track. It also can help sustain motivation, because feedback can be highly reinforcing (Goldstein 1993; Komaki, Collins, and Penn 1982). For example, in a study of self-development groups conducted for students attending a business school, the amount of feedback individuals received from other group members during the last half of the program was one of two factors that predicted success. Improving the change method to enhance feedback increased the percentage of learners who successfully attained their goals from 5 percent to 61 percent (Kolb, Winter, and Berlew 1968). Another, more recent study confirms the value of receiving feedback in learning (Nease, Mudgett, and Quinones 1999).

Feedback is especially useful in social and emotional learning because the learners often have trouble recognizing how their social and emotional behavior manifests itself. In fact, because self-awareness is the core of EI, those who need the most help in emotional competence programs may be particularly weak in this area. For this reason, they need even more focused and sustained feedback as they practice new behaviors.

The amount of practice that is necessary also depends on the competency that is being learned. Improving on a skill that one already possesses requires less sustained practice than changing a deep-seated attitude, value, or personality trait (Spencer, McClelland, and Kelner 1997).

Using Practice and Feedback in the JOBS Program

After participants in this program see a model for how to use a skill, they have ample opportunity to practice it and receive feedback on their performance. For example, job seekers learn how to conduct networking telephone calls by watching the trainers model the wrong way. Then the participants generate ideas and suggestions to improve on the model provided by the trainers. The participants then perform role plays themselves, attempting to incorporate the suggestions made by their peers.

Feedback is provided to the learners at each step of the training process to help them learn the skill and also to enhance their self-confidence. The trainers show the participants how to give one another feedback on their performance by combining positive feedback on what each person did well with suggestions about ways in which he or she can make the performance even better (Vinokur, Price, and Schul 1995).

GUIDELINE 19: INOCULATE AGAINST SETBACKS

Setbacks should not be viewed as signals of defeat. Help learners anticipate and prepare for lapses. After all, learning of a new skill does not proceed in a straight line but in spirals; the learner may fall back on old ways from time to time. This is particularly true at the beginning, when the new way has a feeling of strangeness and unfamiliarity and so demands more intentional effort. The old habit still comes more spontaneously.

Fortunately, a technique—relapse prevention—has proven helpful in preparing people to handle such lapses (Marlatt and Gordon 1985; Marx 1982). The key lies in mental preparation for the slips that are inevitable. The crucial understanding for people attempting to master a competency is that *a slip is not the same as a total relapse.* Since slips are to be expected in the process of mastering any skill, particularly one that requires changing complex habits, people undergoing training need to be told so. By warning people at the outset that there will be times when they will slip back into the old habits and then showing them how to learn from those slips, the trainer can vaccinate the learners against despair. Instead of feeling like giving up, they use the slips as part of their strategy for change.

In relapse prevention training, people are helped to reframe slips as opportunities to learn, thereby reducing the likelihood of slipping again in the future. For dealing with situations in which a mistake is likely, they also are helped to develop practical strategies such as taking a "time out" to consult with a mentor (Kram 1985). Through relapse prevention, learners can identify and overcome potential obstacles as they apply new skills on the job. They also learn to monitor their progress and use methods of self-reinforcement to maintain motivation.

Helping Learners Anticipate Lapses in the Caregiver Support Program

The CSP incorporates relapse prevention throughout the training. At one point, a trainer leads the participants through a discussion about a hypothetical situation in which a participant who has followed all the rules for effective, supportive feedback receives an angry response when talking with a staff member. The trainer then asks the group to describe how they would feel in this situation and to consider what they could do to overcome this particular obstacle. The trainer then praises the participants for their ideas on how to bounce back from this setback. Later, the trainer asks the participants to write on one side of a sheet of paper descriptions of setbacks that they might encounter when they try to apply a skill they have learned. On the other side, they write possible solutions for overcoming these setbacks. The participants then share these strategies with the rest of the group (Heaney, Price, and Rafferty 1995).

Does relapse prevention strengthen people's ability to master emotional competence? Several studies suggest that it does (Gist, Bavetta, and Stevens 1990; Gist, Stevens, and Bavetta 1991; Tziner, Haccoun, and Kadish 1991). Relapse prevention seems to be particularly helpful when learners must apply the new skills in a less-than-supportive environment. For example, in one study conducted at a large firm, supervisory research scientists were trained in such coaching skills as giving feedback. When the learners returned to a climate of fierce work pressure that was, in effect, hostile to their transferring their coaching skills, a full and detailed preparation in relapse prevention was helpful. If their work unit was more supportive of their using the new skills, only a streamlined version of relapse prevention was needed (Burke and Baldwin 1996).

Other studies also point to the interaction of relapse prevention and various elements of training. It may work better when combined, for example, with goal setting and having a coach or trainer who can support people in rethinking how to confront situations that make them vulnerable to slips (Wexley and Baldwin 1986). More than 100 studies have been conducted with people who are trying to change the strongest bad habits of all—drug addiction, alcoholism, overeating, and smoking. These studies show that relapse prevention helps ensure that the habit change will endure (Marlatt and Gordon 1985).

In sum, training and development programs that promise quick and easy improvements—one-day crash seminars to become a better listener or leader, for example—ignore the hard reality that habits change slowly with relapses and slips along the way. Giving people false or unrealistic expectations of the learning process for emotional competence can set them up for a sense of failure when the relapse occurs. Relapse prevention offers a powerful method for helping people turn what may seem a failure into a path to success.

Helping Learners Deal With Lapses in the JOBS Program

Helping learners anticipate and deal with lapses is particularly important in the JOBS program, because job seekers are particularly susceptible to becoming discouraged when they encounter setbacks and barriers. When they do encounter difficulty, they are especially likely to say to themselves, "I'll never be good at networking" or "There just aren't any jobs out there, so what's the use?" This kind of "self-talk" tends to make job seekers depressed and apathetic. The JOBS program thus attempts to generate "methods for helping people build up repertoires of thought and action that can be called upon in the face of setbacks and barriers, slips, and lapses" (Vinokur, Price, and Schul 1995). The trainers encourage participants to list things that could go wrong. Then the participants consider how they would feel (angry, helpless, and so forth) and what they might think ("I knew I'd never be able to do this") if they encounter such barriers. Then, the participants suggest ways for dealing with setbacks and with any accompanying self-defeating thoughts or actions.

The participants are encouraged to realize how responses like these are normal for job seekers. They are told, "These are not personal attacks on the job seeker, but rather responses to a job inquiry." The trainers also work to help the participants reframe these setbacks with the assistance of the other participants. For example, the trainer may reframe a rejection by saying, "One writer has pointed out that successful job seeking is a long string of 'no's' followed by a 'yes.' So the idea is to collect as many 'no's' as possible as quickly as possible in order to reach that 'yes' in the shortest amount of time" (Vinokur, Price, and Schul 1995).

ASSESSMENT QUESTIONS

As you implement EI-based training and development in your organization, consider whether you are addressing the five guidelines of the model's third phase. Ask yourself the following questions:

1. Who will do the training?
2. What will be done to foster a positive relationship between the trainers and learners?

3. Will the trainers have the necessary competencies, especially the emotional and social ones? What will be done to ensure that they do?

4. How can live or videotaped models be used to demonstrate the new competencies in realistic situations?

5. How much time will be spent in experiential activities versus cognitive activities such as lecturing and reading? Will this amount of experiential learning be sufficient?

6. How will learners be encouraged to use naturally arising opportunities for practice of the new competencies?

7. Is the opportunity for practice sufficient to extinguish old habits and make the new competencies automatic for the learners?

8. Do the learners receive enough feedback on their practice efforts?

9. What will be done to help the learners anticipate and prepare for setbacks and lapses?

Phase 4: Encourage, Maintain, and Evaluate Change

Well-designed training programs cannot be effective if the larger organizational system in which they are rooted is not supportive of the training goals. The efficacy of EI training—or any other type of training—can only be gauged through evaluation. That way, weak programs can be improved and effective ones retained. This phase, which comprises three guidelines, indicates ways to help people in EI-based learning programs transfer and maintain change, and it shows how evaluation can be linked to the continual pursuit of high performance.

Transferring and maintaining learned skills is a particular challenge in social and emotional learning. When learners return to their natural environments, many cues and reinforcers are likely to support the old neural pathways that training was designed to weaken. Furthermore, significant barriers may discourage use of some of the new social and emotional competencies that still have fragile neural foundations.

The difficulty of transferring and maintaining social and

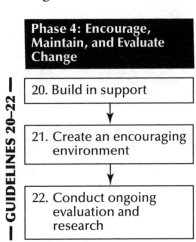

emotional learning was demonstrated in a study of an assertion-training program (Ford 1978). Even though the program was highly effective, gains from the training had disappeared when the participants were tested two months after the training concluded. The author concluded that long-term behavioral maintenance requires special intervention such as training in self-management skills and restructuring the individual's natural environment.

GUIDELINE 20: BUILD IN SUPPORT

Social and emotional training programs are usually more effective when people support each other through the formation of small groups. A substantial body of literature shows how the support provided by self-help groups can be powerful levers for behavioral change (Hinrichsen, Revenson, and Shinn 1985; Levy 1976; Lieberman and Borman 1979; McCrady and Miller 1993; Powell 1994).

"Learning is better maintained if, after training, learners receive support and coaching from valued others (a boss) and from a 'reinforcing reference group' of fellow learners who can support and encourage one another to use the new competency. Ideally training gives the learner membership in a prestigious new group that speaks a new common language, shares new values, and is committed to keeping members' learning alive" (Spencer and Spencer 1993). Such support is especially valuable for people who are trying to improve their social and emotional competence.

Building In Support in the LeaderLab Program

The LeaderLab management development program uses several different processes to support participants as they experiment and change in the emotional and social domains. First, the participants' PAs help them "create and follow through on [their] action plan, coach them through some of the ups and downs of implementing it, and make links between the participants' learnings in LeaderLab and the specific action steps they take back home" (Burnside and Guthrie 1992).

After the first meeting with their PAs, participants speak with their PAs via conference calls every three weeks over the course of four months to discuss further any changes, challenges, or insights they might have regarding their action plans and their own development. This supportive relationship between the participants and process advisors helps encourage and guide the participants' learning experiences. When participants were surveyed after completing the program, they most often mentioned that their PAs, more than anything else, helped them change.

Another support mechanism is the in-class change partner group. The groups are made "as diverse as possible so that participants must learn how to work with people who are different from themselves. As the program evolves, the groups usually become a network of support for their members, and members often use one another as a resource as they work through their action plans during the three months back home" (Burnside and Guthrie 1992).

Participants also establish groups of change partners back in their own work organizations. These individuals provide valuable support during the interval between sessions. The designers of the program viewed it this way: "To be successful, we think the participant must find three things back home: encouragement (someone to commiserate with and prod them); wisdom (someone who has been through similar changes and who knows their local situation); and truth (someone who will give them an honest assessment of the impact of their changes)" (Burnside and Guthrie 1992). Because it is unlikely that one person can provide all of these sources of support, the participants usually include three or four people in their change partner group.

One other support mechanism is LeaderLink, an alumni program that brings participants back to do additional learning. This forum also provides a checkpoint to see where the participants are in their action plans.

Coaches and mentors help sustain a person's hope and motivation. Mentors, in addition to helping people to get ahead, also serve as valuable role models and sources of support. By doing so, they help people develop the social and emotional competencies that are particularly important for success (Fagenson 1989; Kram 1985; Orpen 1995; Scandura 1992). In one training program, the trainers paired up the trainees with someone to provide feedback and encouragement after the training had ended. Data on the program indicated that pairing of trainees led to greater transfer of training (Flemming and Sulzer-Azeroff 1990).

Providing Support in an Executive Coaching Program

Executive and management coaching provides many opportunities to support learners as they struggle to overcome old habits and apply new emotional competencies in their jobs. In the ICE program, the coaching process uses several strategies to support participants in the learning process. First, the coach works as a talent agent, aiding people in the search for various opportunities to use the skills they have acquired in their current work situations. Second, as learners inevitably face moments in their development when they feel stagnant, it is important that coaches work to "manage the mundane components of the development process and work to enhance motivation so that the participant's new skills get used" (Peterson 1996). Third, coaches need to be aware that the fear of failure may prevent learners from taking risks necessary for their skills to flourish. Therefore, they help clients reduce the fear that often arises when they encounter impediments to the use of their new skills on the job.

Relationships at work not only provide support for maintaining learned social and emotional competencies, they also contribute to such learning. For example, in a successful mentoring relationship, the protégé is able to develop greater self-awareness, self-management, and social skills. The mentor, too, can grow socially and emotionally in such relationships (Kram 1996).

Providing Support for Change in Conflict Management Training for Police Officers

One seminal example of conflict management training with police officers began with several weeks of training away from the police academy (Zacker and Bard 1973). To ensure that the training would be reinforced after the recruits began working in real-life settings, all of the trainees who participated in the program were assigned to the same housing projects. The veteran officers working in those projects were reassigned to other projects so that all the officers working in a project would reinforce for one another what had been learned in the training. In addition, the officers received weekly consultation for 12 weeks after formal training. During these consultation sessions, a trainer met with the officers to discuss their experiences in trying to apply what they had learned about dealing with conflict. The trainer provided important support and guidance during these consultations.

GUIDELINE 21: CREATE AN ENCOURAGING ENVIRONMENT

Organizational policies and procedures should reinforce people to work on improving their social and emotional competence. Supervisors also should provide encouragement and support. Help supervisors value and exhibit the competencies, and find ways to integrate emotional competence into the daily activities and culture of the organization.

Change will be greater if the organization's environment—its culture and tone—supports the change and offers a safe atmosphere for experimentation. Programs alone cannot help people upgrade their emotional competence; the organizational climate must reward such effort. For example, resistance to training can come from the grim reality of organizational life; fierce work pressures can prevent people from making the choice to change. When that pattern is rampant in an organization, the first effort needs to go to clearing away these obstacles, creating time for people to begin.

Organizational support, therefore, is important even before people enter a development program, and it remains important throughout the change process and long after it ends. People will be more likely to participate in development efforts, for example, if they perceive them to be worthwhile and effective. The choice to participate in training does not occur in a vacuum. The organization can encourage people to choose to engage in social and emotional learning. Policies and procedures that encourage development activity, combined with supervisor support and training programs that are perceived as worthwhile and effective, enhance trainee motivation (Maurer and Tarulli 1994).

Because social and emotional learning is viewed as "soft" and, therefore, somewhat suspect, employees tend not to choose to participate in it unless they believe that the organization's management strongly endorses it. When management does indicate strong endorsement, employees are likely to be more motivated.

Creating an Encouraging Environment for the Corning Stress Management Program

The developers of the stress management program at Corning encouraged employees to participate in a number of ways. First, they disseminated information about the nature and sources of stress, the mental and physical signs of stress, and the long-term health consequences of stress. "This information was delivered through multiple channels, from simple in-house media communications to formal symposia featuring well-known researchers and personalities, such as Diane Fassel and Art Ulene" (Monroy et al. 1997).

They also tried in various ways to create an environment where it was okay for people to talk about stress and sign up for training. For example, they had a kick-off just to help people become more comfortable with talking about stress as an issue. They also encouraged leaders from various departments to promote the program. They even tried, with some success, to motivate the leaders to attend the workshops and thus model the desired behavior.

The organizers of the program realized that to encourage participation, they needed to help people in the organization overcome the misperception that reducing stress would inevitably reduce productivity. Therefore, they devoted considerable time to educating organizational leaders about the differences between productive and nonproductive stress.

One other way that the organizers encouraged participation was through the program itself. They tried to give the participants many immediately positive experiences, such as exciting demonstrations and fun exercises. It worked. Participants spread the word that the program was enjoyable, and more employees wanted to sign up.

The words and actions of supervisors are especially important. Trainees are more willing to participate in development activity if their supervisors indicate that they support it (Clark, Dobbins, and Ladd 1993; Facteau et al. 1995; Maurer and Tarulli 1994). A study conducted at five companies showed that the more supervisors actively supported an upcoming training session by discussing it with employees, helping them set personal goals, making sure they could take time off, and otherwise encouraging them, the more positive and useful the employees felt the training to be (Cohen 1990).

Likewise, when people enter training with the expectation of a follow-up assessment afterward, they feel more accountable for their learning, and they are more motivated to bring the skills back to their job (Baldwin, Magjuka, and Loher 1991). Yet, surveys of companies show that most simply send employees to training with no systematic follow-up of any kind after they are back at work (Saari et al. 1988).

Credibility is crucial for motivation. People are more likely to participate in development when they trust the person who advises them to do it. The sense that they are being sent to the training by someone who is trustworthy, who understands their unique career goals, who knows the content of the course, and who sees that it would help their prospects within the organization, is a highly motivating combination. That suggests that organizations should be sure that those who "market" a training course to employees has credibility and that the marketing builds a convincing case that the training will help people in their job performance, career prospects, or both.

In general, people are more motivated if they choose their own change goals, but some studies have found that people who are sent for training can be as highly motivated as those who choose to go if they have been given a convincing rationale that shows how the training will help them (Latham, Erez, and Locke 1988). On the other hand, if people are curtly assigned to a training program with no convincing rationale, they are understandably less motivated to go. One common mistake made when introducing emotional competence training into a company is to ignore those very competencies in the process. For example, a major German company hired a consultant to train managers there to be more emotionally intelligent. The top executives who organized the training *commanded* the managers to attend the training. As the consultant put it, "The message was, I order you to become emotionally intelligent by December 1997." Needless to say, huge resistance developed to the program.

When the training ends and people return to their jobs, organizational encouragement and support become even more crucial. Supervisors, peers, subordinates, and others in the work environment can encourage learners in many ways. The best methods involve either reminding people to use the skills or reinforcing them when they do so (Rouillier and Goldstein 1992). For example, when assistant managers who had been through training in managerial skills were randomly assigned to one of 102 units within their organization, the more encouraging the work environment, the more they displayed those skills in their jobs (Rouillier and Goldstein 1991). The most important factors were reminders of their goals that prodded them to use the skills and the implicit encouragement that emanated from their supervisors displaying the abilities.

Reinforcement is a particularly good way to encourage trainees to apply their new skills on the job and to continue doing so. Recognition reinforces efforts to improve, whether in the form of compensation, appreciation from a boss, or other rewards. In some situations, people may receive salary increases in appreciation of their newly developed competence.

On the other hand, a lack of reinforcement discourages lasting change. Indeed, a boss who criticizes, ridicules, or attacks a fledgling competence can extinguish it through the power of punishment. Reinforcement by one's supervisor can be especially powerful (Baldwin and Ford 1988; Noe and Schmitt 1986). Consider the difference in outcomes for two supervisory training programs (Latham and Saari 1979; Russell, Wexley, and Hunter 1984). In both, the participants liked the programs and successfully learned the new skills. Follow-up showed that the participants from the first program applied their skills on the job, while those in the second did not. The biggest difference between the two programs was that the trainees in the first one were "directed and encouraged by their supervisors to use the new skills" (Russell, Wexley, and Hunter 1984). In fact, two of the participants were removed from their jobs for not using the new skills.

Supervisors can reinforce the use of new skills on the job in less drastic ways. They can encourage trainees to use learned skills on the job simply by cueing them to do so (Rouillier and Goldstein 1991). Also, a follow-up assessment of skills learned during training can make the trainees feel more accountable and increase transfer of learning (Baldwin, Magjuka, and Loher 1991). For example, the airlines have "check pilots" who observe flight crews during flights and then give them feedback to encourage the crews to use the teamwork, communication, and leadership skills that they previously learned (Komaki, Heinzmann, and Lawson 1980; Wiener, Kanki, and Helmreich 1993).

Creating an Encouraging Environment for the Emotional Competence Program

The ECT program encouraged participation in a number of ways. Most important, American Express developed a version of the program for the advisors' managers. The company reasoned that if the managers understood what the program was about, they would be more likely to encourage their advisors to participate. Also, when they saw their managers using the program themselves, the advisors would become more receptive to it. The biggest payoff came when the advisors met with their managers for an hour each week to discuss how the advisors were using the emotional competence techniques on the job.

The management version of the program was particularly effective in creating a supportive culture, because whole management teams were trained together. The country was divided into regions, and a team of about 20 individuals, headed by a group vice president, managed each region. Early in the history of the program, the developers offered a version of ECT to entire management teams. The members of a team went through the program together, learning the same concepts, techniques, and language. When they returned to the office, they continued to talk about what they had learned and apply it at meetings, as well as individually.

The ECT developers went on to develop additional versions of the program for other people in the organization: new advisors, experienced advisors, new managers, and for management teams in the corporate office. This way, the developers communicated to all employees that ECT was important and worthwhile. It created a culture in which it was acceptable, even encouraged, to talk about emotions and desirable to become more effective in using them at work.

All of these activities occurred in the context of strong support from top management. Doug Lennick, the senior vice president for sales, spoke in glowing terms about ECT whenever he met with groups of advisors. He told them how important emotional competence had been for him when he was an advisor, and he urged them to take advantage of ECT.

Perhaps most important, top management itself is evaluated in terms of emotional competence. The talent assessment for executives uses a checklist that includes emotional competencies. According to Kate Cannon, who was responsible for ECT at the company, "Each senior vice president completes the checklist on those in a unit, and each vice president does the same on himself or herself. Then they have a dialogue over those areas where they differ. The conclusions are presented to the company president." This appraisal process conveys the message that emotional and social competence "really matters here" (Goleman 1998).

The behavior of a supervisor or any high-status person is important for the transfer and maintenance of new emotional and social competencies. The models to which learners are exposed when they return to the work environment are even more powerful than those they encountered during training. Social and emotional behavior seems to be especially sensitive to modeling effects, and high-status people are influential models for this kind of behavior in the workplace (Manz and Sims 1986; Weiss 1977).

In a classic study, 122 shop supervisors at an International Harvester plant were sent to a two-week training program to promote a more attuned, thoughtful leadership style—one that would make their attitudes toward their workers more "considerate." When they returned to the plant, though, the overriding factor in determining whether their leadership style had become more considerate was not whether they had gone to the training course but whether their *own* boss was a model of considerate behaviors (Fleishman 1955). If the supervisor's boss was autocratic and lacked empathy, then there was no change for the better in the supervisor, regardless of what the training program may have taught. Shop-floor tyrants bred more of the same. If no one (particularly the boss) back at work values an emotional competency, there is likely to be little or no transfer to the job, no matter how stellar the training. That finding, dating from the earliest days of training evaluation in the 1950s, still holds today (Goleman 1998).

How supervisors regard a person's change efforts also matters immensely; people look toward their boss for cues and guidance on how to do their work successfully. Ideally, a boss joins in the effort to master a competency by ensuring that a person has the chance to use the new capability and then gives feedback on how well they do. Those who see that a training program matters to their boss are more motivated, not just to master the emotional competence, but to bring it to their job (Baldwin and Ford 1988).

Although supervisors are especially salient sources of reinforcement and encouragement, other individuals and groups in the work environment can be important, too. Even subordinates can significantly influence learning transfer. For example, in one supervisory skills program, the supervisors' employees were trained at the same time as the supervisors (Sorcher and Spence 1982). This additional component of the program helped create an environment that encouraged the supervisors to practice and use the new behaviors.

In addition to modeling and reinforcement, reflection can help learners transfer and maintain what they have learned. It can be particularly helpful for supervisors to set aside some time periodically to help learners reflect on what they have done to apply the skills and to consider what have been the barriers and facilitating factors. Because self-awareness is a cornerstone of social and emotional competence, reflection can be particularly valuable during the transfer and maintenance phase (Daudelin 1996; Seibert 1996).

Transfer and maintenance of specific skills seems to be affected by the extent to which the organization values learning and development in general (Tracey, Tannenbaum, and Kavanagh 1995). The "learning organization," as described by Senge (1990), represents perhaps the most felicitous environment for encouraging people to keep mastering emotional competencies, rather than stopping after a single attempt. Such settings foster an organization-wide spirit of continuous improvement. The credo of continuous improvement creates the collective expectation that learning matters as part of day-to-day work life. People will continue to upgrade their emotional competencies, along with other relevant skills, if everyone in the organization values and strives for higher levels of work performance as part of a unified effort to help the organization do better. This shared value is in itself a prompt that reinforces EI-based learning and creates a positive feedback loop.

If people believe that their organization appreciates those who engage in continuous improvement of their own and their group's abilities, then people take pride in their efforts. This may mean, for example, not just making people aware of the benefits and payoffs from high levels of emotional competence, but also creating a menu for change so that people see that they have choices readily available. Challenging jobs, social support, reward and development systems, and an emphasis on innovation and competition also encourage learning and development in emotional competence.

The climate of the work environment also affects transfer of social and emotional learning to the job. For example, a European airline offered training in emotional competence to its flight attendants, hoping to boost passenger satisfaction, but independent evaluations showed no effect from the training. The problem might have been the nature of the training, because few of the best-practice guidelines were followed. There was something else, too: the emotional atmosphere at the airline. A bitter labor dispute was on the horizon with threats of strikes by the very people who had been sent through the training. As one executive put it, "The flight attendants feel they're just not valued by management; they haven't gotten raises or bonuses without threatening to strike. They're just not motivated to make the airline look good. Many of them feel malice, even spite. They want to get back at management (Goleman 1998)."

Such an adversarial atmosphere of bitterness offers the worst kind of environment for boosting EI in an organization. A particularly damaging situation arises when employees see training not as an opportunity for themselves, but rather as something imposed solely in the interests of "them" (management) and not "us" (those going through the training).

One study found that participants in a human relations training program who returned to a supportive climate performed better on objective performance measures and were promoted more often than those in an unsupportive climate. Furthermore, these effects were not observed until 18 months after training, highlighting the importance of a supportive environment for the development of social and emotional competencies over time (Hand, Richards, and Slocum 1973).

Therefore, promoting EI means more than just encouraging people to upgrade their human skills; the effort also requires a nurturing environment. An organization that truly supports the significance of emotional competence gets behind these changes by

- offering continuous training programs to people at every level
- using EI as a basis for selection in assessment, recruitment, placement, and promotion
- making EI an operative principle in performance management, succession planning, development, determining career paths, and setting pay scales.

An Encouraging Environment in the Interaction Management Program

For the IMP, managers of the supervisors to be trained attend a workshop that lasts a day and a half. At the workshop they learn many of the essential skills, techniques, and modules that their subordinates will experience during the training. They watch a film, which describes the purpose of the program, and they participate in similar skill modules and skill-practice exercises. "They also are trained in how to work with their subordinate supervisors in diagnosing supervisory problems, in determining the most appropriate interaction skills to use, and in gaining agreements on the desired outcome of the problem situations" (Pesuric and Byham 1996). The workshops also teach the managers how to reinforce their supervisor subordinates when they use the skills on the job.

In another version of this approach, a more supportive culture for learning is created by having line managers serve as workshop leaders. "By using line managers as workshop leaders, the organization built into its reward system a mechanism for communicating to its supervisors that use of the skills was desirable and expected behavior" (Porras and Anderson 1981). In addition, further organizational support was elicited by "introducing top company management to a version of the program." In fact, every manager in the manufacturing division (where the program was implemented) was exposed to "the design's content and process" (Porras and Anderson 1981).

GUIDELINE 22: CONDUCT ONGOING EVALUATION AND RESEARCH

Find unobtrusive ways to measure emotional competence shown on the job. Use these measures to assess the learners before and after training, and also several months later.

Evaluation is essential for promoting effective training. Research suggests that many training programs do not fulfill their promise (Baldwin and Ford 1988). Only through evaluation can poor programs be improved and effective ones retained. Evaluation implies a process that focuses on continuous improvement, not just a pass-fail test in which individuals associated with a program win or lose credibility. When an evaluation suggests that a program fell short of its goals, it should not be used to punish an individual or group. Rather, it should be used as a guide for improving the training that is offered. Evaluation should be linked to learning and the continual pursuit of quality.

Evaluation has received increased attention of late because of the recognition that training departments in modern organizations need to be held accountable (Kraiger and Jung 1997). Instead of cost centers, training departments now are viewed as profit centers. Unfortunately, the field has been slow to meet this challenge. An October 1997 survey of 35 highly regarded "benchmark" companies found that of the 27 companies that said they tried to promote emotional competence through training and development, more than two-thirds made no attempt to evaluate the effect of these efforts. Those that did relied primarily on employee reactions to training (American Society for Training & Development 1997).

That, sad to say, reflects the state of the HR field when it comes to evaluating the effects of most training programs to boost employee competence. A decade before the ASTD finding, another survey of chief training officers at 43 *Fortune* 500 companies found that little rigorous evaluation was conducted of their training programs (Clegg 1987).

Only 15 percent of organizations evaluated training in terms of people's improvement in job performance. Just 8 percent went one step further, evaluating whether there were any improvements in company operating results traceable to training. Most simply took reactions or reviews by participants of the course—whether they liked it or found it well-conducted—as sufficient "evaluation," though such responses say nothing about the worth of the training in terms of on-the-job results.

The most common source of evaluation data was student evaluation sheets, followed by continuing popularity of the training offering. Such assessments are more like popularity polls than hard indicators of performance change. That holds true, too, for the second most common method of training "evaluation": anecdotes and passing comments. Research suggests a zero correlation between trainees' reports of satisfaction and their learning or demonstrated improvement on the job. In other words, "liking does not imply learning" (Tannenbaum and Yukl 1992).

Not a single company routinely used the best, most scientifically sound method for evaluation: pre- and posttraining objective measurement of effects on performance. Ten percent did use such a design on occasion, but most of these evaluation efforts only measured attitude change and not change in on-the-job performance.

Evaluating a Training Program for Supervisors

A training program for supervisors in a large manufacturing plant incorporated measures of both competence improvement and productivity (Porras and Anderson 1981). The evaluators designed a survey instrument that included measures of all the skills targeted in the program, including active listening, use of behavioral descriptions, participative problem solving, positive reinforcement, and action justification. The participants completed surveys one week before the program began, one week after it ended, and six months later. In addition, the surveys were completed by a stratified random sample of 30 percent of the employees reporting to each participant.

Because all the supervisors in one plant received the training, another plant operated by the same company was used as the control. Supervisors and 30 percent of their employees completed the same survey at the same times in the control plant.

The supervisors in the two plants also were compared on a variety of performance indicators before and after the training. Performance measures included average daily production, recovery rate, and production per direct labor worker hours. The evaluators also collected data on labor relations grievances, absenteeism, and turnover.

The results indicated that within two months of the change program, the trained supervisors had significantly increased their use of all five target behaviors. These improvements maintained themselves or increased during the following six months with the exception of action justification, which fell slightly below that of the control group but still remained above initial levels. There also was positive change in several of the performance measures, including increased monthly production, improved recovery rates, and decreased turnover and absenteeism.

Good evaluation of social and emotional learning efforts has been even more rare. One reason seems to be a widespread belief that programs designed to promote soft skills cannot be evaluated. Although this may have been true at one time, the tools are now available to conduct rigorous evaluations of most training programs for social and emotional competence (Goldstein 1993; Spencer, McClelland, and Kelner 1997).

The ideal evaluation design includes a number of features such as sound outcome measures of both the competencies targeted for training and on-the-job performance. Also desirable are pre- and posttraining assessments with follow-up assessments at least several months after the training to be compared to a control group that did not receive the training. Participants for the test and control groups should be randomly assigned. If this ideal is hard to meet, simpler alternatives exist. For example, if it is not possible to have a control group, one can use a multiple baseline design in which several measurements are taken before training begins. Change, then, is determined by comparing the baseline average with the outcomes following training. Another substitute for a control group is to compare change on targeted competencies with change on competencies that were not targeted in the training.

A Company That Takes Evaluation Seriously

Vivendi is a French company with businesses as diverse as telecommunications, energy, mining, and waste management. It has 240,000 employees, 40 percent in Europe, 40 percent in the United States, the rest worldwide. It has a most unusual policy about its training and development programs. "Ten to 15 percent of my training budget is for evaluation of the effectiveness of the programs," says Herve Borensztejn, director of management for Vivendi. "We try to evaluate every training program." The far-flung, separate business units of Vivendi are the training department's internal clients, and they are skeptical consumers. "We need data on the effectiveness of training in order to convince our internal clients to come back to us each year. They have no obligation to use our services," says Borensztejn. When he talked to the Hay/McBer consultants about leadership training for high-potential candidates, part of what he asked for in the training design were pre- and posttraining measures, so that any improvements in the target competencies or business performance could be documented. This request is just part of his routine.

Vivendi also tries to use the most stringent measures for evaluating the company's programs, including return-on-investment. For example, consider how the company evaluates its executive program, an intensive training experience for top managers. The program deals with such topics as leadership and innovation. To evaluate the program, Vivendi looks at all the innovations that are implemented in the subsidiaries managed by the participants after they attend the seminars. Then they calculate the return-on-investment, based on the cost of the training and the value of the innovations.

To ensure that the evaluations are helpful and honest, Vivendi plans to create a steering committee made up of individuals in the company who have competency in the fields of management and training but who are not part of the training and development group. This committee will oversee the evaluation activities and advise the executives who are ultimately responsible for the training and development efforts. "This is the future for HR," Borensztejn predicts. "Internal clients are going to want data showing them they are spending their training and development money wisely" (Borensztejn 1999).

Who does the evaluation is as important as the design. Most evaluations are conducted by the people who do the training (Clegg 1987). Although this may be the most convenient way to get a reading and perhaps serves to give feedback for improvement of teaching, content, or presenters, an obvious problem remains: Those whose jobs depend on the training may be reluctant to take a hard, candid look at how much the training matters for individual or organizational performance. It can be a case of the fox guarding the henhouse (Goleman 1998).

Just how important and valuable a good evaluation can be was demonstrated by the experience of a large pharmaceutical company. The CEO wanted to see how effective the company's training really was, so he commissioned a consulting firm to conduct a study of 11 management training programs that the training department routinely offered (Morrow, Jarrett, and Rupinski 1997). The evaluators used pre- and posttraining assessments of those who went through the programs, and these assessments included ratings of the participants' performance on the job by bosses, peers, and subordinates. They also calculated the costs and benefits of the programs. They found that three of the 11 programs were worthless. On the other hand, five programs had a return-on-investment ranging from 16 to 492 percent, and a time-management program had a return-on-investment of 1,989 percent. The four-year study cost $500,000, which was only 0.2 percent of the $240 million that the company spent on training during that period. As a result of this evaluation, the company eliminated the ineffective programs and retained the ones that more than pay for themselves.

Unfortunately, such rigorous evaluation of a company's training offerings is the exception rather than the rule. Hence, organizations continue to implement programs that are of dubious value to the bottom line. Where is the objective data that shows these training schemes actually improve how well people do their work? As one review of training puts it, despite the sometimes extravagant claims made for them, some programs "tend to be adopted without assessing whether they meet specific instructional needs and without evaluating their effectiveness (Dipboye 1997).

Evaluating Executive Coaching

Executive coaching can be particularly difficult to evaluate because each coaching situation is unique. Peterson (1993) has developed an innovative way to evaluate such programs. The coaching plan rating form serves as the main source of data. This form asks the respondent to rate the individual on a large number of qualities. It is completed by at least three different people: the participant, the participant's boss, and the coach. The raters complete the form just as the program begins and then again at the end of coaching. There also is a follow-up rating that occurs six months later. For the post-coaching and follow-up ratings, the raters gauge the participant's current effectiveness on the job and also the degree of change that has occurred since the previous rating.

The most innovative aspect of this evaluation design is the way that a standard of comparison was developed. Because there cannot be a control group, each participant serves as his or her own control by comparing change on different skills. The control skills are those that are not targeted during the coaching process but that are measured by the coaching plan rating form. These typically are competencies related to finance or written communication. By comparing change on the control items to those that measure program-related content, the evaluator can assess the effectiveness of the intervention. The evaluation data indicates that the average score for the coaching items changes much more than the average score for the control items does.

In companies where many individuals ultimately receive coaching, other analyses can be used, too. In one case, the evaluators compare people who received coaching with those who did not in terms of salary increases. The data indicate that those who received coaching subsequently received higher salary increases than the average employee at the same level.

Fads and fashions will continue, especially in soft skills training, until rigorous evaluation becomes common practice. While it is not always easy to evaluate EI-based training programs, it now is possible to do so with much greater rigor and precision than ever before. By making evaluation an integral part of the process, training programs will gradually become more effective—and accepted. When that happens, everyone wins.

Using Evaluation Research in the Caregiver Support Program

Good evaluation research does more than just indicate whether or not a development program or process has been effective. It also can be used to help trainers and designers to make continual improvements. In the Caregiver Support Program, for example, the program first was pilot-tested with staff from one county in Michigan. "After each session, participants were invited to provide feedback about the relevance and accessibility of the material. Substantial revisions were made in the program based on the comments of these pilot participants. In addition to improving the content of the program, the pilot sessions also provided practice opportunities for the trainers" (Davis-Sacks, Weine, and Heaney 1988).

Once the program became fully operational, the designers continued to monitor it closely to find ways of improving it. Two observers sat in on more than 25 sessions of 11 replications of the program. They wrote a report on their observations with detailed information and recommendations that were incorporated into the intervention redesign. It also helped the evaluators better interpret the data on program outcomes.

The evaluators of this program also looked at how the participants used what they learned in the program and whether they applied the learning on the job. This process evaluation indicated that less than half of the participants had conducted the training activities back in their group homes, which was one of the program's intended outcomes. Nevertheless, 90 percent of the participants had used their newly acquired interpersonal skills back at the group home, and the trained staff were superior to the untrained controls on a number of outcome measures. These results helped the program trainers and designers assess what worked and what did not. They also helped them pinpoint which aspects of the program contributed to the outcomes.

ASSESSMENT QUESTIONS

To maximize the return-on-investment for your organization's training programs, ensure that the learners carry their EI competencies back to the work site, that they apply their new EI competencies, and that the work environment reinforces and encourages the new competencies. Evaluate your programs in terms of return-on-investment. Use the data to improve weak programs, weed out those that are ineffective, and retain those that work. Consider the following questions as you evaluate how well learners apply new social and emotional competencies and gauge the effect of your programs on the bottom line:

1. What will be done to build in support for the learners?
2. Will there be groups, "buddies," coaches, or mentors to help support and reinforce the learners when they return to the work setting?
3. To what extent do organizational policies and procedures encourage people to work on improving their social and emotional competence?
4. What will be done to ensure that the learners' supervisors and other people in the work environment provide the necessary encouragement and support?
5. Will the learners' supervisors possess high levels of the competencies that the learners are developing?
6. How can EI be integrated into the daily activities of the organization?
7. Does the company conduct ongoing evaluation?
8. Does the evaluation include measures of the target competencies and on-the-job performance?
9. Are measures taken pre- and posttraining?
10. Is long-term follow-up conducted?
11. Is there an untrained comparison group or an acceptable alternative, for example, multiple baseline design?

EI

Emotional Intelligence—
The Basis for Success

Emotional intelligence can make the difference between success and failure for both individuals and organizations. It will, however, just become the next trendy idea unless HR managers and practitioners raise the standard. The best-practice guidelines, derived from the model programs, do just that.

SETTING THE STAGE FOR EI-BASED TRAINING

It is possible to become more emotionally intelligent at any point in life. In fact, people naturally do so. Sometimes employers cannot wait for an employee to naturally acquire the competencies necessary for effective performance. In these instances, training and development activities can help speed the process along, but not just any workshop experience will do. People can become more emotionally adept, but the process can be a long and difficult one. Furthermore, the learner must be an active and committed participant. Even the most gifted trainer or mentor cannot do it without the enthusiastic participation of the learner. If learners come into a training experience with the attitude that they will sit back and wait for the trainer to do the work, the result will be little change. If learners fail to apply what they have learned on the job, the result will be little change. If learners practice only in formal training settings and fail to integrate their learning in all areas of their lives, the result will be little change.

Given the challenges associated with bringing about change in the realm of social and emotional competence, one may ask whether it would be better to select for EI than to train for it. In some situations, selection might well be worth considering. Assessment instruments and procedures, such as the behavioral event interview, can help employers select employees who possess the competencies linked to success (Spencer and Spencer 1993). Selection, in many cases, is neither possible nor desirable. Perhaps there are so few candidates for a particular job that the employer cannot find one who has all the competencies necessary for success. Even the best selection process is not be perfect; sometimes the people selected test well but lack one or more emotional competencies necessary for star performance. Rather than fire such employees, who may possess many desirable qualities, employers may wish to help them develop those competencies.

THE BOTTOM LINE

If EI-based training becomes associated with slick, entertaining workshops that make people feel good but that are never shown to improve the bottom line, then the current interest in EI will fade. If EI-based training becomes associated with brief seminars that raise consciousness but do not provide the experiences necessary for true change in social and emotional competence, then the corporate world will soon tire of the topic and move on to something else.

Many HRD professionals already know that the typical soft skills training program is not very effective. They know what needs to be done to change this, but they feel powerless to institute the necessary changes. This book changes all that. Conscientious practitioners now can point to the best-practice guidelines to justify the kinds of well-designed programs that they may have wanted to offer in the past but felt that they could not. In addition, they can point to the bottom-line effects of the model programs to justify the move to EI-based training. The following subsections briefly discuss how the model programs were evaluated and highlight their effects on the organizations in terms of measurable results and the bottom line on their balance sheets.

Achievement Motivation Training

Considerable evaluation research has been conducted on achievement motivation training, and the results are generally positive. One study found that program participants had significantly higher rates of advancement within their companies than did a control group (Aronoff and Litwin 1971). In another evaluation study, an achievement motivation training program that targeted small business owners was effective in influencing business performance as measured by *increased monthly sales, monthly profits, monthly personal income, and number of employees.* Results of a cost-benefit analysis of this government-sponsored program showed that *the net increase in tax revenues due to the increased profitability of the targeted businesses more than paid for the program. After two years the cost-benefit ratio exceeded 5 to 1* (Miron and McClelland 1979).

Caregiver Support Program

This program was evaluated with test and control groups subjected to pre- and posttraining assessments (Heaney, Price, and Rafferty 1995). Group homes initially were randomly assigned to either receive CSP or to serve as controls. Data was collected before the program began and five weeks after training ended. The results showed that direct-care staff who attended the training sessions reported *increased supportive feedback on the job, greater ability to handle disagreements and overload at work, and a better work team climate compared to the controls.*

Emotional Competence Training

Several evaluation studies have been conducted on different versions of ECT at American Express Financial Advisors. The first study looked at the effect of the program on a group of 33 advisors. Prior to their participation, the advisors completed the Seligman Attributional Styles Questionnaire (SASQ), a measure of optimism and coping skill that has predicted success in life insurance sales in previous research. A control group of advisors also completed the questionnaire. The two groups then filled out the questionnaire again after the participants had completed the training. The sales performance of the two groups before and after the training was also compared. The scores of *the trained group increased 13.5 percent on the SASQ* compared to 0.9 percent for the controls. The trained group also showed *larger increases in total sales revenue*—10 percent more than the control group and 16 percent more than the company as a whole. The increase in life insurance sales revenue was even more impressive: *Revenues from the trained group were 20 percent greater than the control group and the company as a whole.*

Another evaluation study examined the effectiveness of a version developed for regional management groups. (These groups supervise the advisors working in a particular region of the country.) This study compared the performance of advisors working under trained managers with those working for managers who had not yet received training. The sales performance of the advisors from both groups was compared for one year prior to and following training. The findings indicated that *advisors working in regions with trained leadership grew their businesses at a rate of 18.1 percent over a period of 15 months compared to a 16.2 percent growth rate for the controls.*

Empathy Training for Medical Students

The program conducted at a large university hospital in Israel (Kramer, Ber, and Moore 1989) was evaluated through pre- and posttraining assessments of test and control groups. Students were randomly assigned to one of four groups:

- a group that received the training
- a group in which the students did not receive training but their tutors participated in a supporting medical-interview workshop
- a group in which both the students and the tutors received training
- a control group that received no training for either students or tutors.

Trained observers watched the students engage in two patient interviews prior to the beginning of the training, during the week following the training, and six and 12 months later. During each 10-minute observation period, the observers recorded how much the students engaged in supporting, neutral, and rejecting behavior.

Results of the evaluation revealed that *students who went through the training showed a significant and lasting increase in supporting behavior,* while students in the control group showed a significant decrease in supporting behavior. Even the tutors who went through the training showed a significant and lasting increase in supportive behavior. However, the students whose tutors went through training but who did not go through the training themselves showed no change in supportive behavior over time.

Executive Coaching

Given the individualized nature of the ICE program, the evaluation research design made use of each participant's individually developed coaching objectives as the primary evaluation measure (Peterson 1993, 1996). Data derived primarily from a coaching plan rating form. This form was completed by the participants, their bosses, and their coaches. The raters filled out the form at entry into the program, at the conclusion of coaching, and about six months after the coaching phase ended. The form included four different types of rating scales: current effectiveness, retrospective degree of change (for the post-coaching and follow-up ratings), global rating scale, and control scale. The last scale was made up of items that were unrelated to the coaching goals and, as such, were not expected to change as a result of coaching. Thus, each participant served as his or her own "control" with changes on targeted behaviors compared to changes on those behaviors not targeted for coaching.

The evaluation revealed that the *participants improved significantly on the targeted behaviors compared to the control-scale items* on the coaching plan rating form. Bosses actually perceived more positive change than did participants. The changes persisted through the six-month follow-up.

Human Relations Training

A rigorous evaluation study of the program occurred when it was implemented in a specialty steel plant located in central Pennsylvania (Hand and Slocum 1972; Hand, Richards, and Slocum 1973). The design involved a comparison of the trained group of managers to a control group that did not receive training. It also involved pretraining, posttraining, and long-term follow-up measures of managerial attitudes, leadership behavior (as perceived by subordinates), and performance (as rated by superiors). The posttraining measures were completed 90 days after training, and the long-term follow-up assessment occurred 18 months after the completion of training.

The results indicated no differences between the two groups at the 90-day posttraining assessment, but several significant differences were noted at the 18-month follow-up. By that time, *the trained managers had become significantly more self-aware and more sensitive to the needs of others* in their attitudes. Their subordinates also perceived them as having *improved in rapport and two-way communication.* The controls, on the other hand, did not change in their attitudes, and their subordinates perceived them as significantly less considerate than they had been at the time of the pretraining assessment. Performance ratings also improved for trained managers working in consultative climates, but not for those working in autocratic climates. In contrast, performance ratings for untrained controls declined over time.

JOBS Program

This program has been evaluated through two large-scale, randomized field experiments. Compared to controls (who received an eight-page booklet with tips on how to find a new job), participants in the program consistently became reemployed more quickly, found higher-quality jobs, and displayed better mental health outcomes. For example, *at the four-month follow-up, 53 percent of the JOBS participants were reemployed compared to 29 percent of the control group.* Results of a follow-up study conducted two and a half years after the JOBS training showed *continued beneficial effects of the program on monthly earnings, level of employment, and episodes of job changes* (Caplan et al. 1989). In addition, cost-benefit analyses show that the economic benefits of the program exceeded its costs. *Four weeks after the program ended, the participants were earning on average $178 per month more than the controls. By four months their earnings were $227 per month higher, and after two and a half years they continued to earn $239 per month more than the controls* (Vinokur et al. 1991).

LeaderLab

This program has been evaluated in several ways (Burnside and Guthrie 1992). One of the evaluations used a retrospective methodology and an impact questionnaire that was completed by both the participants and their co-workers. The impact questionnaire, a 92-item survey clustered into 14 categories related to the various competencies addressed by LeaderLab's training, served as the quantitative outcome measure. It asked the respondents to assess the participant in three ways:

- his or her behavior one year ago
- his or her behavior now
- the effect of the change on the person's effectiveness.

People who had been accepted into the program but had not yet attended also received the impact questionnaire and served as a control group.

Telephone interviews were used as a qualitative measure for gathering action-planning data from the participants, their coworkers, and PAs, three to four months after program completion. The interviews investigated how the participants used their revised action plans after the second session of the program. The data received through this interview process was content-analyzed.

Another set of telephone interviews was conducted three to five months after the program about many aspects of their action plans. Once again, answers to this set of telephone interview questions were content-analyzed.

A comparison of participants to controls on the impact questionnaire showed that *participants significantly improved in eight of the 14 competencies assessed.* These competencies were self-assessment, subordinate development, listening, coping with emotional disequilibrium, interpersonal relationships, flexibility, organizational awareness, and trade-offs. For each of these competencies the difference between the participants and the controls was statistically significant at $p < .01$.

Self-Management Training

This particular self-management program was evaluated with pre- and posttraining assessments of control and experimental groups (Frayne and Latham 1987; Latham and Frayne 1989). Forty individuals initially volunteered for the program and met the eligibility criteria. Half were randomly assigned to receive the training and the other half served as a control group. Outcome measures included trainee reactions, performance on a measure of coping skills, and attendance rates. In addition to a posttraining assessment conducted three months following the training, there were follow-up assessments six and nine months after training.

Results were positive for all three types of outcomes. First, although the trainees initially were hostile to the training—one even accused the trainer of being a spy for management—no one dropped out, and, at the end of the program they rated the training experience very favorably. Second, following the training, the participants scored significantly better than the controls on a test of their ability to come up with solutions to problems affecting attendance.

Most important, the trained employees had significantly better attendance rates following the training. Prior to the training, the employees in the training group clocked an average of 33.1 hours per week (out of a possible 40 hours), and the controls had similar attendance records. *Three months after the training, the trainees had improved to 35 hours per week,* whereas attendance for the controls had dropped slightly. This was a statistically significant change. This difference was maintained: *Six months after training, the trainees' attendance had improved to 38.6 hours per week, and at nine months it was 38.2 hours.* Average weekly attendance was also checked at 12 months for the trained employees, and it remained high at 38.4 hours. Meanwhile, the attendance of the control group remained at the same level during the same nine-month period.

Stress Management Training

A standard symptom checklist was used to evaluate individuals as they went through Corning's stress management program, focusing particularly on weeks 1 (baseline), 8, and 12. The questionnaire assessed the individual's symptoms of stress, stress management skills (the ability to identify stress and to relax), and other life areas (physical exercise). *An analysis of the data comparing weeks 8 and 12 to week 1 revealed significant improvements on measures of stress symptoms, stress management skill, and other life areas.* The largest changes occurred in selected stress symptoms (restlessness, depressed feeling, trouble sleeping, and excessive worry), followed by stress management skills (Monroy et al. 1997).

Similar stress management programs implemented in other settings have been evaluated even more rigorously. Several of the evaluations have used pre- and posttraining assessments of test and control groups with follow-up studies conducted six to 12 months after the programs or even longer. They also have assessed change on a number of different types of outcomes. Several studies, like the Corning one, have shown that *stress management training can produce significant improvements in measures of subjective well-being and physical symptoms* (Backman et al. 1997; Cecil and Forman 1990; Charlesworth, Williams, and Baer 1984; Friedman, Lehrer, and Stevens 1983; Tsai and Crockett 1993). A few studies also have shown that stress management training, of the sort offered at Corning, *can have a positive effect on objective physiological measures* such as electromyograph (Murphy and Sorenson 1988), adrenaline levels (McNulty et al. 1984), and blood pressure (Charlesworth, Williams, and Baer 1984). In one study, a 10-week program for hypertensive employees in a large corporation led to a *sharp cut in medical claims:* The average value of health care claims for the year following the program were half the annual averages for the previous two and a half years (Charlesworth, Williams, and Baer 1984). In another study, a program for highway maintenance workers led to a *significant improvement in attendance* (Murphy and Sorenson 1988). A study involving 44 hospitals found that a comprehensive stress management program led to a *significant reduction in malpractice claims* (Jones et al. 1988).

Training in Conflict Management for Police Officers

To evaluate the efficacy of this pioneering effort to help police officers manage interpersonal conflict (Zacker and Bard 1973), recruits were randomly assigned to one of two groups. One group went through the program. The other group received the same amount of training (42 hours), but the goal was to provide a "well-rounded view of human motivation and behavior," rather than training in specific social and emotional competencies (Zacker and Bard 1973). This alternative training program relied heavily on the traditional lecture format. Topics covered included psychology, sociology, and anthropology. In addition to this "cognitive training" group, the trainees also were compared to a control group of officers who worked in two other housing projects with similar environments and levels of police activity.

The three groups of officers were compared on 10 performance criteria deemed important by police officials: clearance rates (the number of reported incidents divided by the number of arrests for such incidents), total number of arrests, number of misdemeanors, total crime, and a "danger-tension index" (calculated as total arrests divided by total sick days and multiplied by 100). The data was collected and analyzed for each of the housing projects for the year following the training and for the two prior years.

The results indicated that *the housing projects patrolled by the officers who went through the conflict management training showed more improvement on every measured variable.* On the other hand, there was no significant difference between the cognitive training and control groups.

Weatherhead School of Management Program

The competency-based curriculum at the Weatherhead School of Management is being evaluated through a 50-year longitudinal study that will follow the development and careers of its graduates. Both full-time and part-time M.B.A students and professional fellows are involved in this study. Results for students who went through the program have been compared with those of students who previously went through the traditional program. Outcome measures include a critical incident interview exploring the students' effective and ineffective work or school experiences and a videotaped group discussion exercise. These are coded for the competencies that are critical for managerial success, most of which are related to EI. Students also complete the learning skills profile, which is a card-sort of 72 statements of skills related to the individual's levels of skill acquisition and mastery.

Preliminary results suggest that the new competency-based program has resulted in *full-time students improving on 71 percent of the assessed abilities, and part-time students improving on 81 percent of them* (Boyatzis et al. 1996). Furthermore, the competency-based approach has been more effective than the traditional approach used in the past in its effects on social and emotional competence. For example, full-time students in the competency-based M.B.A program experienced a *marked improvement in networking, developing others, self-confidence, oral communication, flexibility, and initiative,* while students in the traditional program improved only in self-confidence. Part-time students in the competency-based M.B.A program increased in initiative, self-confidence, empathy, flexibility, persuasiveness, networking, oral communication, and developing others, whereas part-time students in the traditional program only improved in flexibility.

Another benefit of the new competency based-program is suggested by the *75 percent increase in applications for the full-time program* from the 1989–1990 academic year compared to 1995–1996. This increase occurred at a time when there was a 17 percent decrease in the number of people taking the GMAT, suggesting that the Weatherhead School had increased its appeal at a time when M.B.A programs in general were losing some of their appeal.

MEETING PERSONAL AND BUSINESS GOALS THROUGH EMOTIONAL INTELLIGENCE

Even a cursory review of the bottom-line benefits of the model programs bolsters the movement toward EI-based training. Professionals in the HR field can point to the tangible benefits reaped by the model programs to justify changes in their training programs by incorporating the best-practice guidelines.

The benefits of developing emotional intelligence go far beyond a company's spreadsheets, however. By following the best-practice guidelines presented in this book, HR professionals can help individuals achieve their full potential at work and at home, and by so doing, they can provide a valuable service to their employers, their clients, and, most of all, to society.

Appendix

The Best-Practice Guidelines

PHASE 1: SECURE ORGANIZATIONAL SUPPORT

1. *Move when the timing is right.* Introduce the idea of improving EI when conditions are favorable.

2. *Find a powerful sponsor.* Look for an influential executive who can provide political protection and financial resources for the initiative.

3. *Link EI to a business need.* Show people in the organization that improving EI is not just a nice thing to do but that it makes good business sense.

4. *Recruit emotionally intelligent leadership.* Put the implementation effort in the hands of an individual who has the emotional and social competencies associated with effective leadership.

5. *Give the initiative plenty of autonomy.* The new initiative should be developed in a setting that has a high degree of autonomy and a streamlined mode of operation. An ideal arrangement is a "skunkworks" team that has carte blanche to innovate. The team should have less formality, more flexible roles, and more open flows of information than the usual work group. It also should be kept relatively free of such creativity killers as surveillance, evaluation, micromanagers, and relentless deadlines.

6. *Use research.* Emotional intelligence activities that are not based on solid research are highly vulnerable. Development and evaluation of EI training, even more than other types of programs, needs to be research-driven. The research should be extensive enough to give decision makers confidence that EI training is based on sound, objective analysis.

7. *Maintain high quality.* Because EI training sometimes meets with skepticism, efforts to implement it must be put on a sound footing. If it becomes associated with shoddy, superficial work, resistance will increase. Programs to boost emotional intelligence must be beyond reproach, because opponents of such training need only a few excuses to kill it.

8. *Infuse EI training throughout organization.* To bring EI training into the mainstream, find different ways of inserting EI into the organization. Infusion at many points throughout the organization helps to normalize the concept. It also creates a culture in which people are repeatedly reminded of what they have learned and, therefore, are more likely to apply it on the job.

PHASE 2: PREPARE FOR CHANGE

9. *Assess organizational needs.* Determine the competencies that are most critical for effective job performance in a particular type of job. To do so, use a valid method such as comparison of the behavioral-events interviews of superior performers and average performers. Also, make sure the competencies to be developed are congruent with the organization's culture and overall strategy.

10. *Assess individuals and deliver results with care.* The data should come from multiple sources using several methods to maximize credibility and validity. In delivering the results to the individual, be accurate and clear. Also, allow plenty of time

for the person to digest and integrate the information. Deliver the results in a safe, supportive environment to minimize resistance and defensiveness. On the other hand, avoid making excuses or downplaying the seriousness of deficiencies.

11. *Gauge readiness of learners.* If they are not motivated, make readiness a focus for change. Do not begin training and development until the learners are ready.

12. *Set clear, meaningful, manageable goals.* People need to be clear about what the competence is, how to acquire it, and how to show it on the job. Spell out the specific behaviors and skills that make up the target competency. Make sure that the goals are optimally challenging and broken down into manageable steps.

13. *Make learning self-directed.* People are more motivated to change when they freely choose to do so. To the extent possible, allow people to decide whether or not they will participate in the development process, and have them set the change goals themselves. Let individuals continue to take charge of their learning throughout the program and tailor the training approach to their own learning styles.

14. *Build positive expectations.* Show learners that social and emotional competence can be improved and that such improvement will lead to valued outcomes.

PHASE 3: TRAIN AND DEVELOP

15. *Foster a positive relationship between trainer and learner.* Carefully select trainers based on their warmth, empathy, genuineness, and their ability to relate to the learners, as well as their technical knowledge of the subject and their presentation skills. Give the trainers ongoing evaluation and feedback on these competencies as they lead the training.

16. *Use "live" models.* High-status, highly effective people who embody the competence can be models to inspire change.

17. *Rely on experiential methods.* Emphasize active learning. Spend more time in demonstrations and practice of the competencies than in presenting lectures on them or having learners read about them.

18. *Provide practice and feedback.* Encourage learners to use naturally arising opportunities for practice at work and in life, and to try the new behaviors repeatedly and consistently over a period of months.

19. *Inoculate against setbacks.* Help learners anticipate and prepare for lapses. Use relapse prevention, which helps people use lapses and slip-ups as lessons to prepare themselves better for the next round.

PHASE 4: ENCOURAGE, MAINTAIN, AND EVALUATE CHANGE

20. *Build in support.* Encourage people to form groups to support each other throughout the change effort. Even a single buddy or coach will help.

21. *Create an encouraging environment.* The organization's policies and procedures should reinforce continued improvement of social and emotional competence. Supervisors also should provide encouragement and support. Help supervisors value and exhibit the competencies. Integrate emotional competence into the daily activities and culture of the organization.

22. *Conduct ongoing evaluation and research.* Find unobtrusive measures of the competence or skill as applied on the job, ideally before and after training. Evaluate again at least two months (and again, if possible, a year or more) later.

References

Achenbach, T., and C. Howell. (1989). "Are America's Children's Problems Getting Worse? *Journal of the American Academy of Child and Adolescent Psychiatry, 32* (6), 1145–1154.

Agor, W. (1986). *The Logic of Intuitive Decision-Making.* New York: Quorum Books.

Amabile, T. (1988). "The Intrinsic Motivation Principle of Creativity." In *Research in Organizational Behavior,* B. Staw & L.L. Cummings, editors. Greenwich, CT: JAI Press.

American Society for Training & Development. (1997). *Benchmarking Forum Member-to-Member Survey Results.* Alexandria, VA: Author.

Aronoff, J., and G.H. Litwin. (1971). "Achievement Motivation Training and Executive Advancement." *Journal of Applied Behavioral Science, 7* (2), 215–229.

Bachman, W. (1988). "Nice Guys Finish First: A SYMLOG Analysis of U.S. Naval Commands." In *The SYMLOG Practitioner: Applications of Small Group Research,* R.B. Polley, editor. New York: Praeger.

Backman, L., B.B. Arnetz, D. Levin, and A. Lublin. (1997). "Psychophysiological Effects of Mental Imaging Training for Police Trainees." *Stress Medicine, 13* (1), 43–48.

Baldwin, T.T., and J.K. Ford. (1988). "Transfer of Training: A Review and Directions for Future Research." *Personnel Psychology, 41* (1), 63–105.

Baldwin, T.T., R.J. Magjuka, and B.T. Loher. (1991). "The Perils of Participation: Effects of Choice of Training on Trainee Motivation and Learning." *Personnel Psychology, 44,* 51–65.

Bandura, A. (1977). *Social Learning Theory.* Englewood Cliffs, NJ: Prentice-Hall.

Bandura, A., N. Adams, and J. Beyer. (1977). "Cognitive Processes Mediating Behavioral Change." *Journal of Personality and Social Psychology, 35,* 125–139.

Bandura, A., and D. Cervone. (1983). "Self-Evaluative and Self-Efficacy Mechanisms Governing the Motivational Effects of Goal Systems." *Journal of Personality and Social Psychology, 5* (5), 1017–1028.

Bar-On, R. (1997). *Bar-On Emotional Quotient Inventory: User's Manual.* Toronto: Multi-Health Systems.

Barrick, M., M.K. Mount, and J.P. Strauss. (1993). "Conscientiousness and Performance of Sales Representatives: Test of the Mediating Effects of Goal Setting." *Journal of Applied Psychology, 78* (5), 715–722.

Barsade, S. (1998). *The Ripple Effect: Emotional Contagion in Groups.* New Haven, CT: Yale University School of Management.

Barsade, S., and D.E. Gibson. (1998). "Group Emotion: A View From the Top and Bottom." In *Research on Managing Groups and Teams,* D. Gruenfeld, editor. Greenwich, CT: JAI Press.

Bassett, G.A., and H.H. Meyer. (1968). "Performance Appraisal Based on Self Review." *Personnel Psychology, 21,* 421–430.

Belbin, R.M. (1982). *Management Teams: Why They Succeed or Fail.* London: Halsted Press.

Belbin, R.M. (1996). *Team Roles at Work.* London: Butterworth-Heinemann.

Bennis, W., and P.W. Biederman. (1997). *Organizing Genius.* Reading, MA: Perseus Books.

Borensztejn, H. (1999). Letter to author.

Boyatzis, R.E. (1982). *The Competent Manager: A Model for Effective Performance.* New York: John Wiley and Sons.

Boyatzis, R.E. (1994). "Stimulating Self-Directed Learning Through the Managerial Assessment and Development Course." *Journal of Management Education, 18* (3), 304–323.

Boyatzis, R.E., S.S. Cowen, and D.A. Kolb. (1995). *Innovation in Professional Education: Steps on a Journey to Learning.* San Francisco: Jossey-Bass.

Boyatzis, R.E., D. Goleman, and K.S. Rhee. (In press). "Clustering Competence in Emotional Intelligence: Insights From the Emotional Competence Inventory (ECI)." In *Handbook of Emotional Intelligence,* R. Bar-On & J.D. Parker, editors. San Francisco: Jossey-Bass.

Boyatzis, R.E., D. Leonard, K.S. Rhee, and J.V. Wheeler. (1996). *Combined Faculty Impact on Improving Abilities Through an M.B.A Program.* Cleveland, OH: Weatherhead School of Management, Case Western Reserve University.

Brondolo, E., T. Jelliffe, C.J. Quinn, W. Tunick, and E. Melhado. (1996). "Correlates of Risk for Conflict Among New York City Traffic Agents." In *Violence on the Job: Identifying Risks and Developing Solutions,* G.R. VandenBos & E.Q. Bulatao, editors. Washington, DC: American Psychological Association.

Burke, L., and T. Baldwin. (1996). "Improving Transfer of Training: A Field Investigation of the Effects of Relapse Prevention Training and Transfer Climate on Maintenance Outcomes." Presentation at annual meeting of the Academy of Management, Anaheim, CA.

Burnside, R.M., and V.A. Guthrie. (1992). *Training for Action: A New Approach to Executive Development.* Greensboro, NC: Center for Creative Leadership.

Campbell, D.P. (1990, Spring). "Issues and Observations." *Inklings,* 11–12.

Caplan, R.D., A. Vinokur, and R.H. Price. (1996). "From Job Loss to Reemployment: Field Experiments in Prevention-Focused Coping." In *Primary Prevention Works: Issues in Children's and Families' Lives,* G.W. Albee & T.P. Gullota, editors. Thousand Oaks, CA: Sage.

Caplan, R.D., A. Vinokur, R.H. Price, and M. van Ryn. (1989). "Job Seeking, Reemployment, and Mental Health: A Randomized Field Experiment in Coping With Job Loss." *Journal of Applied Psychology, 74,* 759–769.

Carnevale, A.P., L.J. Gainer, and A.S. Meltzer. (1988). "Workplace Basics: The Skills Employers Want." *Training & Development, 42,* 22–26.

Caruso, B., L.Z. Nieman, and E. Gracely. (1994). "Developing and Assessing the Effectiveness of an HIV Sexual History and Risk Assessment Workshop for Medical Professionals." *Journal of Sex Education and Therapy, 20* (2), 101–109.

Cecil, M.A., and S.G. Forman. (1990). "Effects of Stress Inoculation Training and Co-Worker Support Groups on Teachers' Stress." *Journal of School Psychology, 28* (2), 105–118.

Charlesworth, E.A., B.J. Williams, and P.E. Baer. (1984). "Stress Management at the Worksite for Hypertension: Compliance, Cost-Benefit, Health Care and Hypertension-Related Variables." *Psychosomatic Medicine, 46* (5), 387–397.

Clark, C.S., G.H. Dobbins, and R.T. Ladd. (1993). "Exploratory Field Study of Training Motivation." *Group and Organizational Management, 18* (3), 292–307.

Clegg, W.H. (1987, February). "Management Training Evaluation: An Update." *Training & Development, 41* (2), 65–71.

Cohen, D.J. (1990, November). "What Motivates Trainees?" *Training & Development, 44* (11), 91–93.

Cringely, R.X. (1992). *Accidental Empires: How the Boys of Silicon Valley Make Their Millions, Battle Foreign Competition, and Still Can't Get a Date.* Reading, MA: Addison-Wesley.

Daudelin, M.W. (1996). "Learning From Experience Through Reflection." *Organizational Dynamics, 24* (3), 36–48.

Davis, M., and L. Kraus. (1997). "Personality and Accurate Empathy." In *Empathic Accuracy,* W. Ickes, editor. New York: Guilford Press.

Davis-Sacks, M.L., A. Weine, and C. Heaney. (1988). *The Caregiver Support Program: A Descriptive Account.* Ann Arbor, MI: University of Michigan Prevention Research Center.

Dempster, F.N. (1988). "The Spacing Effect: A Case Study in the Failure to Apply the Results of Psychological Research." *American Psychologist, 43,* 627–634.

Deutsch, M. (1994). "Constructive Conflict Resolution: Principles, Training, and Research." *Journal of Social Issues, 50* (1), 13–32.

Dinella, P. (1999, January 10). Letter to author.

Dipboye, R. (1997). "Organizational Barriers to Implementing a Rational Model of Training." In *Training for a Rapidly Changing Workplace: Applications of Psychological Research,* M.A. Quinones & A. Ehrenstein, editors. Washington, DC: American Psychological Association.

Dowd, K.O., and J. Liedtka. (1994, Winter). "What Corporations Seek in MBA Hires: A Survey." *Selections, 10* (2), 34–39.

Drucker, P.F. (1995). *Managing in a Time of Great Change.* Oxford: Butterworth-Heinemann.

Edelman, G. (1987). *Neural Darwinism: The Theory of Neuronal Group Selection.* New York: Basic Books.

Eden, D. 1990. *Pygmalion in Management.* Lexington, MA: Lexington Books.

Ehringer, A.G. (1995). *Make Up Your Mind.* Santa Monica, CA: Merritt Publishing.

Evans, B.J., R.O. Stanley, R. Mestrovic, and L. Rose. (1991). "Effects of Communication Skills Training on Students' Diagnostic Efficiency." *Medical Education, 25* (6), 517–526.

Facteau, J.D., G.H. Dobbins, J.E.A. Russell, R.T. Ladd, and J.D. Kudisch. (1995). "The Influence of General Perceptions of the Training Environment on Pretraining Motivation and Perceived Training Transfer." *Journal of Management, 21* (1), 1–25.

Fagenson, E. (1989). "The Mentor Advantage: Perceived Career/Job Experiences of Proteges Versus Non-Proteges." *Journal of Organizational Behavior, 10,* 309–320.

Fleishman, E.A. (1955). "Leadership Climate, Human Relations Training, and Supervisory Behavior." *Personnel Psychology, 6,* 205–222.

Flemming, R.K., and B. Sulzer-Azeroff. (1990). "Peer Management: Effects on Staff Teaching Performance." Presentation at 15th Annual Convention of the Association for Behavioral Analysis, Nashville, TN.

Ford, J.D. (1978). "Therapeutic Relationship in Behavior Therapy: An Empirical Analysis." *Journal of Consulting and Clinical Psychology, 46* (6), 1302–1314.

Frayne, C.A., and G.P. Latham. (1987). "Application of Social Learning Theory to Employee Self-Management of Attendance." *Journal of Applied Psychology, 72* (3), 387–392.

Friedman, G.H., B.E. Lehrer, and J.P. Stevens. (1983). "The Effectiveness of Self-Directed and Lecture/Discussion Stress Management Approaches and the Locus of Control of Teachers." *American Educational Research Journal, 20* (4), 563–580.

Friedman, H.S., L.M. Prince, R.E. Riggio, and M.R. DiMatteo. (1980). "Understanding and Assessing Nonverbal Expressiveness:

The Affective Communication Test." *Journal of Personality & Social Psychology, 39* (2), 333–351.

Gist, M.E., A.G. Bavetta, and C.K. Stevens. (1990). "Transfer Training Method: Its Influence on Skill Generalization, Skill Repetition, and Performance Level." *Personnel Psychology, 43,* 501–523.

Gist, M.E., C. Schwoerer, and B. Rosen. (1989). "Effects of Alternative Training Methods on Self-Efficacy and Performance in Computer Training." *Journal of Applied Psychology, 74,* 884–891.

Gist, M.E., C.K. Stevens, and A.G. Bavetta. (1991). "Effects of Self-Efficacy and Post-Training Intervention on the Acquisition and Maintenance of Complex Interpersonal Skills." *Personnel Psychology, 44,* 837–861.

Goldstein, A.P., and M. Sorcher. (1974). *Changing Supervisory Behavior.* New York: Pergamon.

Goldstein, I.L. (1993). *Training in Organizations: Needs Assessment, Development, and Evaluation* (3rd edition). Monterey, CA: Brooks/Cole.

Goleman, D. (1995). *Emotional Intelligence.* New York: Bantam.

Goleman, D. (1998). *Working With Emotional Intelligence.* New York: Bantam.

Greco, M., W. Francis, J. Buckley, A. Brownlea, and J. McGovern. (1998). "Real-Patient Evaluation of Communication Skills Teaching for GP Registrars." *Family Practice, 15* (1), 51–57.

Grencavage, L.M., and J.C. Norcross. (1990). "Where Are the Commonalities Among the Therapeutic Common Factors?" *Professional Psychology: Research and Practice, 21* (5), 372–378.

Hall, D.T. (1976). *Careers in Organizations.* Santa Monica, CA: Goodyear Publishing Co.

Hand, H.H., M.D. Richards, and J.W. Slocum. (1973). "Organizational Climate and the Effectiveness of a Human Relations Training Program." *Academy of Management Journal, 16* (2), 185–195.

Hand, H.H., and J.W. Slocum. (1972). "A Longitudinal Study of the Effects of a Human Relations Training Program on Managerial Effectiveness." *Journal of Applied Psychology, 56* (5), 412–417.

Harris Education Research Council. (1991). *An Assessment of American Education.* New York: Author.

Heaney, C.A., R.H. Price, and J. Rafferty. (1995). "The Caregiver Support Program: An Intervention to Increase Employee Coping Resources and Enhance Mental Health." In *Job Stress Interventions*, L.R. Murphy, J.J.J. Hurrel, S.L. Sauter & G.P. Keita, editors. Washington, DC: American Psychological Association.

Heatherton, T.F., and P.A. Nichols. (1994). "Personal Accounts of Successful Versus Failed Attempts at Life Change." *Personality and Social Psychology Bulletin, 20*, 664–675.

Henry, W.P., T.E. Schacht, and H.H. Strupp. (1986). "Structural Analysis of Social Behavior: Application to a Study of Interpersonal Process in Differential Psychotherapeutic Outcome." *Journal of Consulting and Clinical Psychology, 54* (1), 27–31.

Hicks, W.D., and R.J. Klimoski. (1987). "Entry Into Training Programs and Its Effects on Training Outcomes: A Field Experiment." *Academy of Management Journal, 30*, 542–552.

Hinrichsen, G.A., T.A. Revenson, and M. Shinn. (1985). "Does Self-Help Help? An Empirical Investigation of Scoliosis Peer Support Groups." *Journal of Social Issues, 41* (1), 65–87.

Horvath, A.O., and B.D. Symonds. (1991). "Relation Between Working Alliance and Outcome in Psychotherapy: A Meta-Analysis." *Journal of Counseling Psychology, 38* (2), 139–149.

Howard, A., and Bray, D.W. (1988). *Managerial Lives in Transition.* New York: Guilford Press.

Howard, K., S.M. Kopta, M.S. Krause, and D.E. Orlinsky. (1986). "The Dose-Effect Relationship in Psychotherapy." *American Psychologist, 41* (2), 159–164.

Ilgen, D.R., C.D. Fisher, and M.S. Taylor. (1979). "Consequences of Individual Feedback on Behavior in Organizations." *Journal of Applied Psychology, 64*, 349–371.

Jones, J.W., B.N. Barge, B.D. Steffy, L.M. Fay, L.K. Kunz, and L. J. Wuebker. (1988). "Stress and Medical Malpractice: Organizational Risk Assessment and Intervention." *Journal of Applied Psychology, 73* (4), 727–735.

Kelley, R.E. (1998). *How to Be a Star at Work.* New York: Times Books.

Kluger, A.N., and A. DeNisi. (1996). "The Effects of Feedback Interventions on Performance: A Historical Review, Meta-Analysis, and a Preliminary Feedback Intervention Theory." *Psychological Bulletin, 119* (2), 254–284.

Kolb, D.A., and R. Boyatzis. (1970). "Goal-Setting and Self-Directed Behavior Change." *Human Relations, 23* (5), 439–457.

Kolb, D.A., S.K. Winter, and D.E. Berlew. (1968). "Self-Directed Change: Two Studies." *Journal of Applied Behavioral Science, 4,* 453–471.

Komaki, J.L., R.L. Collins, and P. Penn. (1982). "The Role of Performance Antecedents and Consequences in Work Motivation." *Journal of Applied Psychology, 67,* 334–340.

Komaki, J., A.T. Heinzmann, and L. Lawson. (1980). "Effect of Training and Feedback: Component Analysis of a Behavioral Safety Program." *Journal of Applied Psychology, 65,* 261–270.

Korsgaard, M., and M. Diddams. (1996). "The Effect of Process Feedback and Task Complexity on Personal Goals, Information Searching, and Performance Improvement." *Journal of Applied Social Psychology, 26,* 1889–1911.

Kosslyn, S.M., and O. Koenig. (1995). *Wet Mind: The New Cognitive Neuroscience.* New York: Free Press.

Kraiger, K., and K.M. Jung. (1997). "Linking Training Objectives to Evaluation Criteria." In *Training for a Rapidly Changing Workforce: Applications of Psychological Research,* M.A. Quinones & A. Ehrenstein, editors. Washington, DC: American Psychological Association.

Kram, K.E. (1985). "Improving the Mentoring Process." *Training & Development, 39,* 40–43.

Kram, K.E. (1996). "A Relational Approach to Career Development." In *The Career Is Dead—Long Live the Career,* D.T. Hall, editor. San Francisco: Jossey-Bass.

Kramer, D., R. Ber, and M. Moore. (1989). "Increasing Empathy Among Medical Students." *Medical Education, 23,* 168–173.

Lansing, A. (1959). *Endurance: Shackleton's Incredible Voyage.* New York: Carroll and Graf.

Latham, G.P., and L.M. Saari. (1979). "Application of Social-Learning Theory to Training Supervisors Through Behavioral Modeling." *Journal of Applied Psychology, 64,* 239–246.

Latham, G.P., M. Erez, and E.A. Locke. (1988). "Resolving Scientific Disputes by the Joint Design of Crucial Experiments by the Antagonists: Application to the EREZ-Latham Dispute Regarding

Participation in Goal-Setting." *Journal of Applied Psychology, 73* (4), 753–772.

Latham, G.P., and C.A. Frayne. (1989). "Self-Management Training for Increasing Job Attendance: A Follow-Up and a Replication." *Journal of Applied Psychology, 74* (3), 411–416.

LeaderLab. (1994). "Creative Leadership in Action: LeaderLab Program Manual." Greensboro, NC: Center for Creative Leadership.

LeFevre, J. (1988). "Flow and Quality of Experience During Work and Leisure." In *Optimal Experience: Psychological Studies of Flow in Consciousness,* M. Csikszentmihalyi & I.S. Csikszentmihalyi, editors. New York: Cambridge University Press.

Leslie, J.B, and E. van Velsor. (1996). *A Look at Derailment Today: North America and Europe.* Greensboro, NC: Center for Creative Leadership.

Levinson, W., D.L. Roter, J.P. Mullooly, and V.T. Dull. (1997). "Physician-Patient Communication: The Relationship With Malpractice Claims Among Primary Care Physicians and Surgeons." *Journal of the American Medical Association, 277* (7), 553–559.

Levy, L.H. (1976). "Self-Help Groups: Types and Psychological Processes." *Journal of Applied Behavioral Science, 12,* 310–322.

Lieberman, M.A., and L. Borman. (1979). *Self-Help Groups for Coping with Crises: Origins, Members, Processes, and Impact.* San Francisco: Jossey-Bass.

Locke, E.A., and G.P. Latham. (1990). *A Theory of Goal Setting and Task Performance.* Englewood Cliffs, NJ: Prentice-Hall.

Lusch, R.F., and R. Serpkenci. (1990). "Personal Differences, Job Tension, Job Outcomes, and Store Performance: A Study of Retail Managers." *Journal of Marketing, 54* (1), 85–101.

Magjuka, R.J., T.T. Baldwin, and B.T. Loher. (1994). "The Combined Effects of Three Pretraining Strategies on Motivation and Performance: An Empirical Exploration." *Journal of Managerial Issues, 17,* 282–296.

Manz, C.C., and H.P. Sims, Jr. (1986). "Beyond Imitation: Complex Behavioral and Affective Linkages Resulting From Exposure to Leadership Training Models." *Journal of Applied Psychology, 71,* 571–578.

Marlatt, A., and J. Gordon. (1985). *Relapse Prevention.* New York: Guilford Press.

Marx, R.B. (1982). "Relapse Prevention for Managerial Training: A Model for Maintenance of Behavior Change." *Academy of Management Journal, 35,* 828–847.

Mason, J.L., S.E. Barkley, M.M. Kappelman, D.E. Carter, and W.V. Beachy. (1988). "Evaluation of a Self-Instructional Method for Improving Doctor-Patient Communication." *Journal of Medical Education, 63,* 629–635.

Maurer, T.J., and B.A. Tarulli. (1994). "Investigation of Perceived Environment, Perceived Outcome, and Person Variables in Relationships to Voluntary Development Activity by Employees." *Journal of Applied Psychology, 79* (1), 3–14.

Mayer, J.D., P. Salovey, and D. Caruso. (1998). "Competing Models of Emotional Intelligence." In *Handbook of Human Intelligence,* R.J. Sternberg, editor. New York: Cambridge University Press.

McCall, M., and M. Lombardo. (1983). *Off the Track: Why and How Successful Executives Get Derailed.* Greensboro, NC: Center for Creative Leadership.

McClelland, D.C. (1998). "Identifying Competencies With Behavioral-Event Interviews." *Psychological Science, 9* (5), 331–339.

McCrady, B.S., and W.R. Miller. (1993). *Research on Alcoholics Anonymous: Opportunities and Alternatives.* New Brunswick, NJ: Rutgers Center for Alcohol Studies.

McNulty, S., D. Jeffreys, G. Singer, and L. Singer. (1984). "Use of Hormone Analysis in the Assessment of the Efficacy of Stress Management Training in Police Recruits." *Journal of Police Science and Administration, 12* (2), 130–132.

Miller, W.R., R.G. Benefield, and J.S. Tonigan. (1993). "Enhancing Motivation for Change in Problem Drinking: A Controlled Comparison of Two Therapist Styles." *Journal of Consulting and Clinical Psychology, 61* (3), 455–461.

Miller, W.R., and S. Rollnick. (1991). "Principles of Motivational Interviewing." In *Motivational Interviewing: Preparing People to Change Addictive Behavior,* W.R. Miller & S. Rollnick, editors. New York: Guilford Press.

Miron, D., and D.C. McClelland. (1979). "The Impact of Achievement Motivation Training on Small Businesses." *California Management Review, 21* (4), 13–28.

Monroy, J., H. Jonas, J. Mathey, and L. Murphy. (1997). "Holistic Stress Management at Corning." In *The New Organizational Reality: Downsizing, Restructuring, and Revitalization,* M.K. Gowing, J. Quick & J.D. Kraft, editors. Washington, DC: American Psychological Association.

Moreland, R.L., L. Argote, and R. Krishnan. (1998). "Training People to Work in Groups." In *Theory and Research on Small Groups,* R.S. Tindale, R. Scott & L. Heath, editors. New York: Plenum.

Morrow, C.C., M.Q. Jarrett, and M.T Rupinski. (1997). "An Investigation of the Effect and Economic Utility of Corporate-wide Training." *Personnel Psychology, 50,* 91–119.

Murphy, L.R., and S. Sorenson. (1988). "Employee Behaviors Before and After Stress Management." *Journal of Organizational Behavior, 9,* 173–182.

Nease, A.A., B.O. Mudgett, and M.A. Quinones. (1999). "Relationships Among Feedback Sign, Self-Efficacy, and Acceptance of Performance Feedback." *Journal of Applied Psychology, 84* (5), 806–814.

Noe, R.A, and N. Schmitt. (1986). "The Influence of Trainee Attitudes on Training Effectiveness: Test of a Model." *Personnel Psychology, 39,* 497–523.

Orpen, C. (1995). "The Effects of Mentoring on Employees' Career Success." *Journal of Social Psychology, 135,* 667–668.

Pesuric, A., and W. Byham. (1996, July). "The New Look in Behavior Modeling." *Training & Development, 50* (7), 25–33.

Peterson, D.B. (1993). "Skill Learning and Behavior Change in an Individually Tailored Management Coaching Program." Presentation at annual conference of the Society for Industrial and Organizational Psychology, San Francisco, CA.

Peterson, D.B. (1996). "Executive Coaching at Work: The Art of One-on-One Change." *Consulting Psychology Journal, 48* (2), 78–86.

Peterson, D.B., S.W. Uranowitz, and M.D. Hicks. (1996). "Management Coaching at Work: Current Practices in *Fortune*

250 companies." Presentation at annual conference of the American Psychological Association, Toronto.

Pilling, B.K., and S. Eroglu. (1994, Winter). "An Empirical Examination of the Impact of Salesperson Empathy and Professionalism and Merchandise Salability on Retail Buyers' Evaluations." *Journal of Personal Selling and Sales Management,* *14* (1), 55–58.

Porras, J.I., and B. Anderson. (1981). "Improving Managerial Effectiveness Through Modeling-Based Training." *Organizational Dynamics, 9,* 60–77.

Powell, T.J. (1994). *Understanding Self-Help: Frameworks and Findings.* Newbury Park, CA: Sage.

Price, R.H., and A.D. Vinokur. (1995). "Supporting Career Transitions in a Time of Organizational Downsizing: The Michigan JOBS Program." In *Employees, Careers, and Job Creation,* M. London, editor. San Francisco: Jossey-Bass.

Prochaska, J.O., J.C. Norcross, and C.C. DiClemente. (1994). *Changing for Good: The Revolutionary Program That Explains the Six Stages of Change and Teaches You How to Free Yourself From Bad Habits.* New York: W. Morrow.

Quinones, Miguel A. (1996). "Contextual Influences on Training Effectiveness." In *Training for a Rapidly Changing Workforce: Applications of Psychological Research,* M.A. Quinones & A. Ehrenstein, editors. Washington, DC: American Psychological Association.

Richman, L.S. (1994, May 16). "How to Get Ahead in America." *Fortune,* 46–54.

Robins, C.J., and A.M. Hayes. (1993). "An Appraisal of Cognitive Therapy." *Journal of Consulting and Clinical Psychology, 61* (2), 205–214.

Rosier, R.H., and P. Jeffrey, editors. (1994). *The Competence Model Handbook* (Volume 1). Boston: Linkage Incorporated.

Rosier, R.H., and P. Jeffrey, editors. (1995). *The Competence Model Handbook* (Volume 2). Boston: Linkage Incorporated.

Roter, D., J. Rosenbaum, B. de Negri, D. Renaud, L. DiPrete-Brown, and O. Hernandez. (1998). "The Effects of a Continuing

Medical Education Programme in Interpersonal Communication Skills on Doctor Practice and Patient Satisfaction in Trinidad and Tobago." *Medical Education, 32* (2), 181–189.

Rouillier, J.Z., and I.L. Goldstein. (1991). "Determinants of the Climate for Transfer of Training." Presentation at annual meeting of the Society for Industrial and Organizational Psychology, New Orleans.

Rouillier, J.Z., and I.L. Goldstein. (1992). "The Relationship Between Organizational Transfer Climate and Positive Transfer of Training." *Human Resource Development Quarterly, 4* (4), 377–390.

Russell, J.S., K.N. Wexley, and J.E. Hunter. (1984). "Questioning the Effectiveness of Behavior Modeling Training in an Industrial Setting." *Personnel Psychology, 37,* 465–481.

Ryman, D.H., and R.J. Biersner. (1975). "Attitudes Predictive of Diving Training Success." *Personnel Psychology, 28,* 181–188.

Saari, L.M., T.R. Johnson, S.D. McLaughlin, and D.M. Zimmerle. (1988). "A Survey of Management Training and Education Practices in U.S. Companies." *Personnel Psychology, 41* (4), 731–743.

Saks, A.M. (1995). "Longitudinal Field Investigation of the Moderating and Mediating Effects of Self-Efficacy on the Relationship Between Training and Newcomer Adjustment." *Journal of Applied Psychology, 80* (2), 211–225.

Sawyer, J. (1999). "New-Hire Sales Training: Integrating Work and Learning." In *Performance Interventions: Selecting, Implementing, and Evaluating the Results,* B. Sugrue and J. Fuller, editors. Alexandria, VA: American Society for Training & Development.

Scandura, T. (1992.) "Mentorship and Career Mobility: An Empirical Investigation." *Journal of Organizational Behavior, (13),* 169–174.

Schulman, P. (1995). "Explanatory Style and Achievement in School and Work." In *Explanatory Style,* G. Buchanan and M.E.P. Seligman, editors. Hillsdale, NJ: Lawrence Erlbaum.

Scott, B. (2000). *Consulting on the Inside: An Internal Consultant's Guide to Living and Working Inside Organizations.* Alexandria, VA: American Society for Training & Development.

Seibert, K. (1996). "Experience Is the Best Teacher, If You Can Learn From It: Real-Time Reflection and Development." In *The Career Is Dead: Long Live the Career,* D.T. Hall, editor. San Francisco: Jossey-Bass.

Senge, P. (1990). *The Fifth Discipline.* New York: Doubleday/Currency.

Snyder, C.R. (1993). *The Psychology of Hope.* New York: Free Press.

Sonne, J.L., and D. Janoff. (1982). "The Effect of Treatment Attributions on the Maintenance of Weight Reduction: A Replication and Extension." *Cognitive Therapy & Research, 3,* 389–397.

Sorcher, M., and R. Spence. (1982). "The InterFace Project: Behavior Modeling as Social Technology in South Africa." *Personnel Psychology, 35,* 557–581.

Spencer, L.M., Jr. (1997, July). "Computing ROI's in Training and Development Efforts." Presentation at International Family Business Programs Association, Northampton, MA.

Spencer, L.M., Jr., and C.C. Morrow. (1996). "The Economic Value of Competence: Measuring ROI." Presentation at Conference on Using Competence-Based Tools to Enhance Organizational Performance, Boston, MA.

Spencer, L.M., Jr., D.C. McClelland, and S. Kelner. (1997). "Competency Assessment Methods: History and State of the Art." In *What Works: Assessment, Development, and Measurement,* L.J. Bassi & D. Russ-Eft, editors. Alexandria, VA: American Society for Training & Development.

Spencer, L.M., Jr., and S. Spencer. (1993). *Competence at Work: Models for Superior Performance.* New York: John Wiley & Sons.

Sweeney, P. (1999, February 14). "Teaching New Hires to Feel at Home." *New York Times.*

Tannenbaum, S.I., and G. Yukl. (1992). "Training and Development in Work Organizations." *Annual Review of Psychology, 43,* 399–441.

Tobin, D. (2000). *All Learning Is Self-Directed.* Alexandria, VA: American Society for Training & Development.

Tracey, J.B., S.I. Tannenbaum, and M.J. Kavanagh. (1995). "Applying Trained Skills on the Job: The Importance of the Work Environment." *Journal of Applied Psychology, 80* (2), 239–252.

Tsai, S-L., and M.S. Crockett. (1993). "Effects of Relaxation Training, Combining Imagery and Meditation, on the Stress Level of Chinese Nurses Working in Modern Hospitals in Taiwan." *Issues in Mental Health Nursing, 14,* 51–66.

Tziner, A., R.R. Haccoun, and A. Kadish. (1991). "Personal and Situational Characteristics Influencing the Effectiveness of Transfer of Training Improvement Strategies." *Journal of Occupational Psychology, 64,* 167–177.

U.S. Office of Personnel Management. (1996). *Mosaic Competencies for Professionals and Administrators.* Washington, DC: Author.

Vinokur, A.D., R.H. Price, and Y. Schul. (1995). "Impact of the JOBS Intervention on Unemployed Workers Varying in Risks for Depression." *American Journal of Community Psychology, 23* (1), 39–74.

Vinokur, A.D., and Y. Schul. (1997). "Mastery and Inoculation Against Setbacks as Active Ingredients in the JOBS Intervention for the Unemployed." *Journal of Clinical and Consulting Psychology, 65,* 867–877.

Vinokur, A.D., M. van Ryn, E.M. Gramlich, and R.H. Price. (1991). "Long-Term Follow-Up and Benefit-Cost Analysis of the JOBS Program: A Preventive Intervention for the Unemployed." *Journal of Applied Psychology, 76,* 213–219.

Walter V. Clarke Associates. (1996). *Activity Vector Analysis: Some Applications to the Concept of Emotional Intelligence.* Pittsburgh, PA: Author.

Wasielewski, P.L. (1985). "The Emotional Basis of Charisma." *Symbolic Interaction, 8* (2), 207–222.

Weiss, H.M. (1977). "Subordinate Imitation of Supervisor Behavior: The Role of Modeling in Organizational Socialization." *Organizational Behavior and Human Performance, 19,* 89–105.

Wexley, K.N., and T.T. Baldwin. (1986). "Posttraining Strategies for Facilitation of Positive Transfer: An Empirical Exploration." *Academy of Management Review, 29,* 503–520.

Wiener, E.L., B.G. Kanki, and R.L. Helmreich. (1993). *Cockpit Resource Management.* New York: Academic Press.

Williams, W.M, and R. Sternberg. (1988). "Group Intelligence: Why Some Groups Are Better Than Others." *Intelligence, 12* (4), 351–377.

Young, D.P., and N.M. Dixon. (1996). *Helping Leaders Take Effective Action: A Program Evaluation.* Greensboro, NC: Center for Creative Leadership.

Zacker, J., and M. Bard. (1973). "Effects of Conflict Management Training on Police Performance." *Journal of Applied Psychology, 58* (2), 202–208.

For Further Reading

Burke, M., and R. Day. (1986). "A Cumulative Study of the Effectiveness of Managerial Training." *Journal of Applied Psychology, 71,* 232–245.

Falcone, A.J., J.E. Edwards, and R.R. Day. (1986). "Meta-Analysis of Personnel Training Techniques for Three Populations." Presentation at annual meeting of the Academy of Management, Chicago, IL.

Hunter, J.E., F.L. Schmidt, and M.K. Judiesch. (1990). "Individual Differences in Output Variability as a Function of Job Complexity." *Journal of Applied Psychology, 75,* 28–42.

About the Authors

CARY CHERNISS

Cary Cherniss is a professor of applied psychology at Rutgers, The State University of New Jersey, and co-chair of the Consortium for Research on Emotional Intelligence in Organizations. He received his doctorate from Yale University in 1972 and specializes in the areas of emotional intelligence, work stress, burnout, leadership training and development, planned organizational change, and career development. He has published many scholarly articles and is the author of several other books: *The Human Side of Corporate Competitiveness,* with Daniel Fishman, *Professional Burnout in Human Service Organizations, Staff Burnout,* and *Beyond Burnout: Helping Teachers, Nurses, Therapists, and Lawyers Recover From Stress and Disillusionment.* He has also consulted with many organizations in the public and private sectors including American Express, Johnson & Johnson, AT&T, Bellcore, Colgate Palmolive, the U.S. Office of Personnel Management, and the Marriott Corporation.

MITCHEL ADLER

Mitchel Adler holds a master's degree of psychology and is currently pursuing a doctorate in the department of clinical psychology at the graduate school of applied and professional psychology (GSAPP) at Rutgers, The State University of New Jersey. He was the recipient of the GSAPP scholars' award, the graduate scholars' award, and the first GSAPP alumni scholarship. The subjects of his scholarly investigation include judgment and decision making as they pertain to individuals, groups, and organizations; the relationship between social and emotional competence and subjective well-being; and program planning and evaluation. As a research assistant with the Consortium for Research on Emotional Intelligence in Organizations, he aided in the creation of the consortium's technical report (available on the consortium's Website at www.eiconsortium.org). Working primarily with adults and adolescents, he combines organizational and clinical theory into his writing, consulting, and psychotherapy work.